Mallorca

Front cover: the cove of Portals Vells

Right: Miro's *Personatge* sculpture in Palma de Mallorca

TOP 10 ATTRACTIONS

Sa Calobra • A glorious bay at the end of a long and winding road *(page 58)*

Beaches • The island's beautiful beaches, lapped by clear waters, are the biggest attractions for many visitors

Traditional windmills • Many on the Central Plain have been renovated and put back into use *(page 69)*

Deià • Once the home of Robert Graves and still one of the prettiest villages on the island *(page 52)*

The Orange Tram • This rattles between Sóller and its port as it has done for many decades *(page 54)*

Port de Pollença • One of the most popular family resorts in Mallorca *(page 63)*

Cala Figuera • This lovely place is still a working fishing port *(page 80)*

Palma's cathedral • Dominating the city and the harbour, this marvellous Gothic cathedral is a stunning sight *(page 29)*

The Gran Hotel • Now a cultural centre, this is one of the finest examples of the Moderniste style *(page 35)*

A PERFECT DAY

9.00am Breakfast

In Palma, have breakfast in the ornate interior of the Art Nouveau Bar Cristal in Plaça de Espanya, where elderly waiters treat customers with the deference that would have been the norm when the bar was established.

1.00pm Delightful Deià

Continue on the scenic coast road to Deià, a honey-coloured little town that was home to poet Robert Graves and still attracts writers and artists. Wander round the picturesque streets and browse in the boutiques.

12 noon Sweet treat

Explore town and stop for coffee and a coca de patata, a sweet local pastry, in the Carrer Blanquera.

2.00pm Graves's grave

Take a break for tapas in El Barrigon Xelini, a huge and atmospheric bar on the main road, with a pleasant outside terrace. Afterwards visit the poet's simple grave in the hilltop cemetery and his home, Ca N'Alluny, now a small museum.

10.00am In search of Chopin

Take the road that runs about 10km (6 miles) through groves of olive and almonds to Valldemossa and La Real Cartuja, where you can visit the apartments in which George Sand and Frédéric Chopin lived for a winter. In the adjoining palace, Palau del Rei Sanxo, recitals of Chopin's music are held at intervals throughout the day.

CONTENTS

IN MALLORCA

6.00pm Spectacular sunset

Make your way back down the coast a few kilometres to Son Marroig, home to a 19th-century Austrian archduke who fell in love with the island. You can visit his house and gardens (open till 8pm) but the main attraction is having a drink in the on-site bar and watching the spectacular sunset over the sea and the rocky promontory called Na Foradada.

11.00pm Nightlife

Back in Palma, take a gentle stroll along the harbour, then, if you have the energy, indulge in a cocktail in the exotic surroundings of Abaco, in Carrer Sant Joan, in the old town.

3.30pm The beach

Take a 35-minute walk through olive and lemon groves (or opt for a 2-km/1-mile drive) to the Cala de Deià, a pretty little rocky cove where you can swim and sunbathe.

8.00pm A choice of dining

Drive the short distance back the way you came for dinner in one of Deià's excellent restaurants. Go up-market with nouvelle cuisine at El Olivo (part of La Residencia hotel, tel: 971 639 011)), or stay more down to earth with excellent home cooking at Jaume (tel: 971 639 029), on the main road. Both need advance booking.

62

73

75

INTRODUCTION

Mallorca could claim to be the perfect holiday island, blessed with attributes that entice millions of foreign visitors annually. Many of them return year after year, sometimes to the second homes they bought when they first fell in love with the island, or the boats they keep moored in one of the many harbours. The deep blue and translucent turquoise of the Mediterranean, hundreds of kilometres of coastline, secluded rocky coves and wide sandy beaches, a vibrant and sophisticated capital city, some 300 days of brilliant sunshine each year and a vast choice of accommodation and cheap flights make it irresistible.

A Varied Landscape

Lying off the northeast coast of Spain, Mallorca is the largest of the five Balearic Islands, but it is not a big place. It has more than 550km (325 miles) of coastline, but at its widest point – Cap de Sa Mola in the southwest to Capdepera in the northeast – it is only 100km (60 miles) across; at its narrowest, from the Badia d'Alcúdia in the north to the Badia de Palma in the south, it's only half that distance.

> **Blue Flag beaches**
>
> Mallorca's beaches gained a bad reputation at one time, but after a major clean-up campaign no fewer than 34 beaches and six marinas have been awarded the coveted Blue Flag for safety and cleanliness.

The landscape, however, is extremely varied. The dramatic cliffs edging the Serra de Tramuntana hug the west coast from Andratx all the way to Cap de Formentor. The coastal scenery is stunning, with dizzying drops to the sea and the tiny

Old windmill at Felanitx, in the southeast of the island

coves far below and picturesque villages set among centuries-old terraces. To the northwest, away from the coast, the Tramuntana range provides ideal walking and climbing conditions. There are 10 main peaks in the range, the highest of which is Puig Major at 1,445m (4,741ft). The north coast is dominated by the Bay of Alcúdia – 12km (8 miles) of fine golden sand sloping into shallow waters – and by the grassy wetlands of S'Albufera, now a protected natural park. The interior is a vast plain with sleepy towns, sandstone churches, well-tended farmland, groves of ancient olive trees and orchards of almonds and apricots. On the east coast, long sweeps of beach alternate with intimate little coves and spectacular cave formations, while several picturesque fishing harbours retain their individuality. The south centres on the cosmopolitan capital, Palma, with its splendid bay. Around it, to the east and west, spread the crowded beaches whose glorious sands first brought mass tourism to the island in the late 1950s.

Views along the west coast

Climate

Mallorca's climate is heavenly for northern Europeans. Although summer extremes of 34°C (93°F) can be uncomfortable, the July–August average is a pleasant 24° (76°F); winters are mild and not too wet, and even the timid can swim in the sea from June to October.

Vegetation and Birdlife

The flora of the island is as diverse as the landscape. There are cultivated olives, almonds, apricot and citrus trees; holm oaks and pines flourish in mountainous regions, with rosemary, lavender and heather turning the hillsides purple. There are sturdy palm trees growing at sea level, and bougainvillaea brightening village walls; and there are wild orchids and water-loving reeds, sedges and poplars in the S'Albufera marshes.

Lemons ripe for picking

Mallorca is rich in birdlife. Come in spring, as so many bird-watchers do, to see the numerous migrants who find Mallorca a convenient stopping-off place. The Boquer Valley, near Pollença, is popular with those in the know. S'Albufera, on the north coast, plays host to numerous resident and migrant species, including the cattle egrets that can be seen standing on the backs of cows, pecking insects from their hides, and birds such as Eleanor's falcons that spend the summer here. Among the most colourful and exotic birds that can be seen in many locations in summer are bee-eaters and hoopoes. The island of Cabrera and the Parc Natural de Mondragó in the southeast corner are among the best places to spot migrating seabirds.

The Islanders and Their Language

The population of Mallorca is approximately 628,000, of whom more than half – 325,000 – live in the capital. The rest are distributed across 53 municipal districts, with the in-

Catching up on the news

terior plain being the most sparsely populated region. In the peak summer season, tourists – some 9 million a year, mostly German and English – and hordes of seasonal workers, many from Andalusia, swell the population and strain the infrastructure and water supply to their limits.

Mallorcans are bilingual in Spanish and in Mallorquí, a variant of Catalan, which is now the official language. Most signs and street names are written in Mallorquí, and this is the language people choose to speak among themselves, and which is used in schools. However, they are a communicative people, quite happy to address outsiders in Castilian (Spanish), and the high number of seasonal workers from the mainland ensures that Spanish is spoken everywhere.

Tourism Trends

Mallorca was one of the first places in Spain to be developed for tourism in the 1950s. Ever since, it has been one of the major centres, and tourism is now responsible for nearly 90 percent of the island's income. But the industry has had contradictory effects. Income from it made this region Spain's wealthiest per capita, but the environmental and psychological effects of being Europe's low-budget playground have taken a heavy toll. Four decades after it exploded, tourism overheated, leaving a forest of towering hotels and beach-hugging villa communities, whole resorts lined with fast-food outlets, tourist tat shops and loud clubs and bars serving dangerously cheap alcohol, with the big 'M' of McDonald's looming over the commercial centres.

In the 1990s, the island government realised it was time to reassess Mallorca's tourism industry. Fearing that massive over-development and the increasingly bad reputation earned by the raucous behaviour of some visitors, as well as new trends in international tourism, were leaving the Balearics behind, the authorities took action. Moves were made to protect the remaining undeveloped areas as nature preserves, proclaiming them off-limits to construction, and demolishing some of the more unsightly hotel complexes. Almost one third of the island is now under some kind of protection order, and the advantages to the landscape and wildlife are palpable.

There have also been energetic moves to encourage a more up-market and environmentally friendly kind of tourism. The

Magaluf was among the first of the large-scale resorts

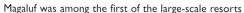

View across the island from the Puig de Randa

government's *agroturisme* initiative, which promotes accommodation in small rural hotels and *fincas* (farmhouses) has been extremely popular, both with visitors looking for peace and quiet amid scenic surroundings, and farming families who were struggling to keep their properties going *(see page 114 for details)*.

Walking paths have been opened up and clearly marked, and a number of hilltop sanctuaries provide rest and respite for walkers; natural parks are widely promoted and user-friendly; and considerable investment has gone into golf courses and marinas, to attract higher income tourists and improve the environment.

In Palma de Mallorca, guided walking tours around the convents, palaces and the waterfront encourage visitors to appreciate the city's heritage, while the diversity and the quality of the capital's many museums and cultural centres would be pretty impressive in a city twice the size.

Enjoying the Island

Throughout the island, summer music festivals are held in beautiful historic buildings, attracting internationally known performers, while traditional, local festivals are also being promoted as a way of disseminating the rural culture of the Balearics. There has also been a renewed interest of late in Mallorcan food, *cuina Mallorquina*, and many venues, from the traditional *cellers (see page 72)* to smart restaurants and more basic establishments are finding that local people and foreign visitors alike are enjoying what they have to offer.

Mallorca is not a difficult place to get around. Obviously, hiring a car gives you most freedom, and this is relatively inexpensive and stress free, as most roads (except the stretch around the Bay of Palma) don't get too busy, even in summer, and parking (once you're away from the capital) is not a huge problem. But public transport is good, too: there are regular buses from Palma to most points of interest (some services are more limited on Sundays), and two railway lines – one of which makes the scenic journey on the narrow-gauge line to Sóller *(see page 53)*. For another aspect of the island, you can take boat trips round many parts of the coast.

A girl wears traditional dress at a village festival

With all this going for it, Mallorca cannot be regarded as simply a place for sun, sea and sand holidays – but there is no denying that sun, sea and sand are still excellent reasons to come here.

A BRIEF HISTORY

Many influences have shaped Mallorca over the past 4000 years and helped make it the fascinating place it is today. The stone towers called *talayots* that can still be seen in parts of the island were defensive structures built by early inhabitants, who are believed to have made settlements here around 1300BC. Even before that, neolithic islanders had graduated from cave dwellings to simple stone houses and cleared fields by piling stones into dividing walls – the origins of the intricate dry-stone walls called *parets seques* or *margers* that can still be seen in the island interior.

Over the centuries, the inhabitants traded with the Phoenicians, Carthaginians and Greeks, and the Carthaginians gradually colonised the islands (c. 400BC), absorbed them into

The *talayotic* settlement at Ses Païsses

their trading empire and founded the main ports. But by 123BC the Romans, who had pacified most of Spain, despatched an invading force to conquer the islands, which they named Balearis Major (Mallorca) and Balearis Minor (Menorca).

Romans, Vandals and Moorish Occupation

The Romans introduced the Christian religion, constructed roads and established the towns of Palmaria (Palma) and Pollentia (near Alcúdia), but during the 5th century AD, as the Roman Empire crumbled, Goths, Vandals and Visigoths poured into the Balearics. The Vandals destroyed almost all evidence of Roman occupation – the remains of Pollentia outside Alcúdia are among the very few traces left – before they were ousted in AD534 by a Byzantine expedition from Constantinople.

But more invaders were to follow. Ignited by the teachings of the Prophet Mohammed, Islam spread like wildfire in the 8th century. A Moorish army led by General Tarik landed on the Iberian peninsula in 711 and in just seven years, most of Spain was under Moorish rule. While the Balearics remained submissive, the *caliphs* (rulers) were content to accept tribute from them, but local disturbances prompted an invasion at the beginning of the 10th century. Both islands were conquered and became part of the Caliphate of Córdoba.

Although little Moorish architecture remains – the Arab Baths in Palma and the Jardins d'Alfàbia near Sóller are two

---

Balearic slingers

The early inhabitants' skill with stones was evident in their deadly use of the slingshot. The 'Balearic slingers' were renowned throughout the Mediterranean world and recruited by Hannibal to fight for the Carthaginians in the Punic Wars against Rome. The name Balearic probably comes from the Greek word, *ballein*, 'to throw'.

The Banys Àrabs in Palma

exceptions – the influence can be seen in Palma, in the Palau de l'Almudaina, in the fountains in S'Hort del Rei, and in many shady patios. Some place names are also of Arabic origin – Alcúdia (Al-Kudia) means 'on the hill', and Binissalem means 'son of peace'.

The Reconquest

The aim of the crusades in Spain was the eviction of the Muslims. After the recovery of Jerusalem in 1099, it took 400 years of sieges and battles, treaties and betrayals before Christian rulers succeeded in subduing the Moors. In 1229, a Catalan army led by King Jaume I of Aragón and Catalunya took Mallorca. Jaume proved to be an enlightened ruler who profited from the talents of the Moors – those who remained were forcibly converted to Christianity – as well as those of the large Jewish and Genoese trading communities.

Jaume I reigned in Aragón for six decades, but he made the mistake of dividing between his sons the lands he had united. Initially this resulted in the Independent Kingdom of Mallorca, first under Jaume II, then under Sanxo and Jaume III. But dynastic rivalry triggered the overthrow of the latter by his cousin, Pere IV. Attempting to make a comeback, Jaume III was killed in battle near Llucmajor in 1349.

In the following century the Catholic Monarchs, Ferdinand and Isabella, leading a unified Spain, completed the Reconquest, taking Granada, the only Moorish enclave left on the peninsula, in 1492.

The Spanish Empire

As one tumultuous age ended, another began. Christopher Columbus (Cristobal Colón), the seafaring captain from Genoa (whom at least three Mallorcan towns claim as their own), believed he could reach the East Indies by sailing westwards. In the same year that Granada fell, Columbus crossed the Atlantic. Spain exported its adventurers, traders and priests, and imposed its language, culture and religion on the New World, creating a vast empire in the Americas. Ruthless, avaricious conquistadors extracted and sent back incalculable riches in the form of silver and gold. The century and a half after 1492 was known as Spain's Golden Age, but it carried the seeds of its own decline. Plagued by corruption and incompetence, and drained of manpower and ships by such adventurism as the dispatch of the ill-fated Armada against England in 1588, Spain was unable to defend her expansive interests.

Jaume I, who captured Mallorca in 1229

The Balearic Islands did not benefit much from Spain's glory years. They were forbidden to trade with the New World, and their existing trade on the eastern routes was interrupted by marauding pirates based in North Africa, as well as by the powerful Turkish fleet.

Wars and Consequences

Ferdinand and Isabella greet Christopher Columbus

The daughter of Ferdinand and Isabella married the heir to the Holy Roman Emperor, Maximilian of Habsburg. The Spanish crown duly passed to the Habsburgs and remained in their hands until the feeble-minded Carlos II died in 1700, leaving no heir. France seized the chance to install the young grandson of Louis XIV on the Spanish throne. A rival Habsburg claimant was supported by Austria and Britain, who saw a powerful Spanish-French alliance as a major threat. In the subsequent War of the Spanish Succession (1702–13) most of the kingdom of Aragón, including the Balearics, backed the Habsburgs. Britain seized Menorca and retained it, under the Treaty of Utrecht, when the war was over.

By 1805, Spain was once more aligned with France, and Spanish ships fought alongside the French against Admiral Lord Nelson at the Battle of Trafalgar. But Napoleon came to distrust his Spanish ally and forcibly replaced the king of Spain with his own brother, Joseph Bonaparte. A French army marched in to subdue the country. The Spanish resisted and, aided by British troops commanded by the Duke of Wellington, drove the French out. What the British call the Peninsular War (1808–14) is known in Spain as the War of Independence.

During the 19th century, most of Spain's possessions in the Americas broke away. The Balearics, further neglected, were beset with poverty and thousands of islanders emigrated to South America in search of a better life. A brief upturn, due to the successful trade in wine, ended when the phylloxera louse destroyed the island's vines.

Crises, Republic and Civil War

The beginning of the 20th century in Spain was marked by social and political crises, assassinations and near anarchy. The colonial war in Morocco provided a distraction, but a disastrous defeat there in 1921 led to a coup and the dictatorship of General Primo de Rivera. He fell in 1929, and when elections of 1931 revealed massive anti-royalist feeling, the king followed him into exile.

The new republic was conceived amid an outbreak of strikes and uprisings. In February 1936 the left-wing Popular Front won a majority of seats in the Cortes (parliament), but across Spain localised violence displaced debate. In July 1936, General Francisco Franco staged a coup, which was supported by the military, monarchists, conservatives, the clergy and the right-wing Falangist movement. Aligned on

Creative Input

Mallorca has always attracted creative people. In 1838 Frédéric Chopin and George Sand spent several months in Valldemossa, during which he composed *The Raindrop Prelude* and she wrote *A Winter in Majorca*. Catalan poet and painter Santiago Rusinyol spent some time in Deià at the turn of the 20th century; and poet and author Robert Graves came to the village in 1929 and made it his home. He was buried in the little churchyard on the hill in 1985; his son, Tomás, still lives on the island. Artist Joan Miró, whose wife Pilar was Mallorcan, set up house and studio in Palma in 1956, rather than live under the Franco regime and he, too, stayed until his death (in 1983).

the Republican government's side were liberals, socialists, communists and anarchists. The ensuing Spanish Civil War (1936–39) was brutal and bitter. Support for both sides poured in from outside Spain. Those on the Republican side believed it was a contest between democracy and dictatorship, while Nationalist supporters saw it as a battle between order and communist chaos. During the three years the war lasted, around one million Spaniards lost their lives.

Mallorca and Menorca found themselves on opposite sides. Menorca declared for the Republic, and stayed with it to the bitter end. Mallorca's garrison seized the island for the Nationalists. Early in the war, the Republicans used their one battleship to support an invasion of Mallorca, but it ended in failure. A decisive factor was the presence in Palma of Italian air squadrons, used to bomb Republican Barcelona.

New Horizons

Exhausted after the Civil War, Spain remained on the sidelines during World War II and, after the dark years of isolation known as the *Noche Negra* (Black Night), began a slow economic recovery under Franco's oppressive, law-and-order regime, boosted by the growth of the tourism industry.

A small élite had visited the island in the 1920s, but it was in the late 1950s and early 1960s that northern Europeans began making sun-seeking pilgrimages to Spain, and the Balearic Islands, in any numbers. Tourism transformed the impoverished country's economy, landscape and society. Eager to capitalise, government and private interests poured everything into mass tourism, triggering a rash of uncontrolled and indiscriminate building, with scant regard for tradition or aesthetics. Almost as influential as the financial input, to a country that had for so long been cut off from the rest of Europe, was the injection of foreign influences, particularly those associated with the liberalism of the 1960s.

Mallorca, once dependent on agriculture, fishing and small local industries, experienced an explosive growth in tourism and swiftly became one of Europe's most popular holiday destinations.

After the death of General Franco in 1975, his designated successor, the grandson of Alfonso XIII, was crowned King Juan Carlos I. To the dismay of diehard Franco supporters, the king managed a smooth transition to democracy, then stood back to allow it full rein, as he continues to do today. After decades of repression, new freedoms and autonomy were granted to the Spanish regions and their languages and cultures enjoyed a long-sought renaissance. The Balearic Islands were granted a degree of autonomy in 1978 and five years later became the Comunidad Autónoma de las Islas Baleares. Mallorquí was recognised officially as the language of Mallorca.

The Spanish and Balearic flags fly side by side

Street music is a part of many traditional occasions

Modernisation

Spain joined the European Community (now the European Union) in 1986, which gave a further boost to an expanding economy. Mallorca's tourist industry continued to grow but so did a realisation that lack of planning and good taste were leading to damaging long-term consequences – to the environment and to the island's reputation. By the late 1990s, when the lager lout image had become too closely associated with some resorts, production of domestic waste was double the national average and electricity consumption had increased by 37 percent in five years, a new emphasis on quality tourism and safeguarding the environment had taken root. Building restrictions were implemented and a substantial number of areas were declared protected zones (see page 13).

A current economic concern is that tourists are spurning Mallorca in favour of cheaper destinations; and the worldwide economic downturn affected the island's tourist industry in 2009, when visitor numbers, in the early part of the season at least, were down substantially. It is to be hoped that the international situation will improve, and that in Mallorca a balance will be achieved: sufficient visitors to boost the economy, but not so many that the island's distinctive character is submerged. Coupled with the new environmental awareness, and the legislation to back it up, this will preserve the natural beauty and friendly atmosphere of this lovely island.

Historical Landmarks

c. 1300BC Megalithic Talayotic culture; stone towers, *talayots*, built.

c. 400BC Carthaginians colonise the Balearics.

123BC–AD400 Romans invade; they name the island Balearis Major and establish towns, including Palmaria (Palma) and Pollentia (Alcúdia).

426 Vandals invade Balearics.

711 Moors land near Gibraltar, and Spain falls under Islamic rule.

848 Moorish rule imposed in the Balearics; it lasts for 300 years.

1229 Mallorca taken by the Christian army under Jaume I.

1285–87 Alfonso III of Aragón captures Palma.

1349 Jaume III killed in battle by Pere IV of Aragón, ending the Independent Kingdom of Mallorca.

1492 Spain united under the Catholic Monarchs.

1554 Palma fortified to protect it from pirate attacks.

1713 Juníper Serra, founder of the Californian missions, born in Petra.

1837 First steamship service links Mallorca and Spanish mainland.

1936–39 Spanish Civil War. Mallorca seized by Nationalist forces.

1936–75 Franco's dictatorship; economic hardship in the early years.

1960 Mallorca's airport built. Tourism begins to replace agriculture as the island's main source of income.

1975 Juan Carlos I becomes king after the death of Franco.

1978 Statute of Autonomy gives the Balearic Islands a degree of autonomy; five years later they become an autonomous province and Catalan/Mallorquí is restored as the official language.

1986 Spain joins the European Community (now European Union).

1996 The government of the Balearic Islands initiates measures to protect the environment and encourage eco-friendly tourism.

2002 The euro becomes the official currency.

2004 PSOE (Socialist Party) comes to power in Spanish elections but Partido Popular (PP) is dominant in the Balearic Islands.

2006–7 Mallorcan government continues efforts to move tourism upmarket, encouraging agro-tourism. Rural and boutique hotels flourish.

2009 Tourist industry affected by worldwide economic downturn.

WHERE TO GO

Although some visitors to this small Mediterranean island arrive by ferry from mainland Spain, the majority land at Palma's airport, Son Sant Joan, 9km (5½ miles) outside the capital, Palma de Mallorca. A ring road – the Via Cintura – skirts the city, with roads radiating off to the rest of the island; to the craggy, beautiful northwest coast, the quiet, friendly towns of the interior plain, the wetlands of S'Albufera in the north, the tiny calas in the east, and the tourist-dominated strips to the east and west of Palma and along the north coast.

Tour agencies offer excursions, by coach or boat, or a combination of the two, to hidden beaches, mountain villages, spectacular caves and weekly markets, but hiring a car *(see page 117)* is the best way to get around. There are only two rail lines – one goes to Inca (with some trains continuing to Sineu), in the centre of the island, the other is the picturesque route to Sóller *(see page 53)*, but bus services throughout Mallorca are comprehensive and reliable *(see page 130)*, although they obviously give you less freedom than a hired car.

PALMA DE MALLORCA

Set around a sheltered bay, **Palma** is a large, cosmopolitan city, with around 325,000 inhabitants – over half the permanent population of Mallorca. It is very much a Mediterranean city, with palm trees and bushes of fragrant oleander, outdoor cafés with colourful awnings, and yachts bobbing in the bay among working vessels. Palma is a city with a long history, too, as the Gothic cathedral towering above the city walls indicates as you approach from the airport. It's smart

Sant Elm, with the island of Sa Dragonera

and urbane, with designer boutiques, smart restaurants and chic art galleries hidden in narrow alleys. And it's a city that stays awake late at night. Every visitor should try to spend a whole day here, at least, but it really merits a longer stay.

The old quarter surrounding the cathedral – 'Centre Historic' on direction signs – sits on a small hill overlooking the bay, and its narrow, atmospheric streets are full of pleasant surprises. To the east of the centre is the Platja de Palma, a long line of excellent sandy beaches that have been defaced by a stretch of concrete from Ca'n Pastilla to S'Arenal. To the west is the seaside promenade of modern Palma, where luxury hotels look out over a forest of masts in the yacht harbour, although divided from it by a stretch of six-lane highway. Crowning the wooded slopes above the city, where the Spanish royal family have a summer home, are the stone towers of the Castell de Bellver *(see page 41)*.

Palma's cathedral keeps watch over the harbour

The Cathedral

Standing proudly above the city walls, spectacular when illuminated at night, is the  **Cathedral** (Jun–Sept: Mon–Fri 10am–6.15pm; Apr–May/Oct: till 5.15pm; Nov–Mar till 3.15pm; Sat 10am–2.15pm all year; charge; entered via the museum). Also known as **La Seu**, this is one of the finest Gothic churches in the whole of Spain. Begun in 1230 by Jaume I, on the site of the Great Mosque after the Christians recaptured

Cathedral tower by night

the island from the Moors, it took nearly four centuries to complete. Densely packed flying buttresses on the south front create an extraordinary effect, especially in the glow of the setting sun when they are reflected in the lake of the Parc de la Mar below.

The 14th-century **Portal del Mirador** on this same front is a feast of carved stone figurines by architect and sculptor Guillem Sagrera (1397–1454), including a depiction of the Last Supper. Entry via the Portal de l'Almoina, below the square, 13th-century bell tower, is reserved for those attending mass. Before you go in, stop to admire the splendid view of the Bay of Palma from the **Mirador** the to the south.

The **Museu del Catedral** (hours as above) contains a splendid silver monstrance, some interesting medieval paintings and holy relics. Sections of the original Roman city can be seen through a glass floor. An early Renaissance doorway in carved stone leads into the baroque Chapter House. The vault of the cathedral's three-aisled, 121-m (396-ft) interior

Guided tours

In summer, a number of guided tours cover aspects such as Modernisme, the Jewish Quarter, a night tour, and one called Palma Monumental that gives a good historical background. Pick up leaflets from one of the tourist offices, or contact tel: 902 102 365.

is supported by slim, elegant pillars. The largest of the seven **rose windows** is magnificent, 12m (40ft) across, composed of 1,236 separate sections of stained glass. The extraordinary *baldachino*, a wrought-iron crown of thorns over the high altar, was added by Catalan *Moderniste* architect Antoni Gaudí, creator of Barcelona's Sagrada Família, who worked for 10 years on the cathedral in the early 20th century. (*Modernisme* is the Catalan version of art nouveau.) The tombs of Jaume II and Jaume III, 14th-century kings of Catalunya and Mallorca, are in the Capella de la Trinitá at the east end. And St Peter's chapel is covered with innovative ceramics by Mallorcan artist Miquel Barceló, on which he worked for six years before it was unveiled in February 2007.

To the east of the Cathedral is the **Museu Diocesà** (Mon–Sat 10am–2pm; charge), back in its permanent home in the Episcopal Palace. It contains medieval and Gothic statuary along with some lovely stained-glass windows by Gaudí, who lived in the palace while he worked on the Cathedral. The palace itself is well worth a look, as well.

Palau de l'Almudaina

🅑▶ The **Palau de l'Almudaina** (Apr–Sept: Mon–Fri 10am–5.45pm, Sat 10am–1.15pm; Oct–Mar: 10am–1.15pm, 4–5.15pm; charge) stands to the west of the cathedral. Once the residence of the Moorish viziers, then of the medieval kings of Mallorca, it is a perfect blend of Islamic and Catalan-Gothic architecture. There is a stone-vaulted, 13th-century throne room (the Tinell), a pretty courtyard (Patio del Rei), a Gothic chapel (Capella de Santa Anna), and heavily restored royal offices, sometimes used by the present king, where traces of early paintwork survive on the ceilings and walls. There are also some impressive 15th- and 16th-century Flemish tapestries.

The 18-m (58-ft) **Arc de la Drassana Musulmana** spanning the water in S'Hort del Rei below *(see page 38)* once gave the Moorish rulers direct access to the sea.

Around the Historic Centre

In Carrer Palau Reial, to the north of the Almudaina, where brightly painted horse-drawn carriages wait for customers, is another palace, which houses the **Palau March Museu** (Apr–Oct: Mon–Fri 10–6.30pm; Nov–Mar: till 5pm; Sat 10am–2pm all year; charge). Within this majestic building and its

The Palau de l'Almudaina was home to medieval kings

Sculpture at Palau March

courtyard a small but superb collection of contemporary sculpture has been gathered, including works by Henry Moore, Barbara Hepworth, Rodin and Chillida, and murals by the Catalan artist Josep Maria Sert, as well as high-quality temporary exhibitions. The palace is also a venue for classical concerts in July and August *(see page 93)*.

The ochre colonnades of the Parliament Building – **Parlament de les Illes Baleares** – run almost the length of Carrer Palau Reial. At the far end, the opulent Renaissance facade of the **Ajuntament** (Town Hall), its overhanging wooden roof supported by carved beams, dominates the **Plaça del Cort**. (You can go inside to see the huge processional figures that are stored here.) In the centre of the square is an ancient, gnarled olive tree, a favourite spot for photos.

Turn right from the *plaça* and you will reach a pleasant little square, named for the 14th-century church of **Santa Eulàlia**, which has a Gothic nave, altar paintings by Francisco Gomez and several baroque chapels. Behind the church in the narrow Carrer Can Sanç (off Carrer Carnisseria) is **Can Joan de S'Aigo** (closed Tue), a beautifully tiled café, founded in 1700, which was artist Joan Miró's favourite place for hot chocolate and almond cake.

A right turn brings you to Plaça Quadrado, shaded by palms and plane trees, and with a number of attractive *Moderniste* buildings, the best one being Can Barceló (1902). Above the third-storey oriel windows the facade is decorated with mosaics portraying domestic scenes with

women and children. The massive 13th-century **Basílica**
de Sant Francesc (Mon–Sat 9.30am–12.30pm, 3.30–6pm;
charge) backs onto Quadrado, and dominates the adjoining Plaça Sant Francesc. A sculpture outside depicts Mallorcan missionary, Fray Juníper Serra, founder of the first
Californian missions *(see page 71)*. To the left of the
baroque altar a chapel contains the alabaster tomb of Catalan scholar, mystic and missionary, Ramón Llull (1235–
1316). But the main event is the enchanting Gothic cloister (through which you enter the church), with slender
columns, delicate tracery and lemon trees around a central
fountain – peaceful except when children from the adjacent
school use it at break times.

Basilica de Sant Francesc

Patios and Museums

The old quarter of Palma is
rich in baronial mansions,
most dating from the 16th–
18th centuries, with won-
derful patios behind their
great wooden doors. With
ornate staircases, decorated
tiles, palms and potted
plants, sometimes cooled by
small fountains, they are a
delight. Among the best are
Can Olesa on Carrer Morey,
Can Tacón on Carrer de
Sant Jaume II, and Can Bor-
dils and Can Oms, both on
Carrer Almudaina.

Most are private or com-
mercial properties and you
have to be content with

peeping through the gateways. You can, however, see several of these patios by visiting the museums housed within. On Carrer de la Portella, the Renaissance **Ca La Gran Cristiana** houses the **Museu de Mallorca** (Jun–Oct: Tue–Sat 10am–7pm, Sun 10am–2pm; free; currently undergoing essential building work). The basement has excellent exhibits on the *talyotic* period, there are 13th–16th-century religious paintings displayed on the first floor, and *Moderniste* tiles and 20th-century paintings and sculpture on the floor above.

Another splendid mansion with a patio in Carrer de la Portella is home to the **Casa Museu Torrents Lladó** (mid-Jun–mid-Sept: Tue–Fri 11am–7pm; winter: 10am–6pm; Sat 10am–2pm all year; charge). The beautifully furnished home and studio of the 20th-century Catalan portraitist and landscape painter is fascinating, and houses an eclectic selection of his work and memorabilia.

The only private mansion that can be visited is **Can Marquès** (Mon–Fri 10am–3pm; charge), in nearby Carrer Zanglada. Originally 15th-century, the house is mostly furnished and decorated in bourgeois, 19th-century style, with some interesting *Moderniste* additions; a guided tour illuminates the lifestyle of an upper-class Mallorquin family of the period.

Inside Can Marquès

Not far away, on Carrer Can Serra, are the **Banys Àrabs** (Arab Baths; Apr–Nov: daily 9am–7.30pm; Dec–Mar: 9am–6pm; charge), still standing after 1,000 years. The courtyard garden is a tranquil, beautiful place when it's not filled with excursion groups. Late afternoon is a good time to go.

Moderniste Sites

Alternatively, retrace your steps to Plaça Cort, from where it's a short distance up the intriguing little shopping streets of Carrer Colom and Jaume II to the deep yellow facades and green shutters of the former market place, the **Plaça Major**. The square is busy with cafés, street entertainers and handicraft stalls selling scarves, jewellery and batik work. Escalators lead down to a subterranean shopping mall and public toilets.

Gran Hotel

Approaching the square, you pass the **Plaça Marquès del Palmer** where there are two excellent examples of *Moderniste* architecture – Can Forteza Rei and L'Àguila, adorned with ornate iron grillwork and colourful ceramic flourishes; a café and a smart shoe shop occupy the ground floors.

Down a flight of steps from the Plaça Major, lined with tourist-trap kiosks, is Plaça Weyler, with two more fine examples of *Modernisme*. The major one is the imposing **Gran Hotel**, now run as a cultural centre by the **Fundació La Caixa** (Tue–Sat 10am–9pm, Sun 10am–2pm; free). It includes a bookshop, a smart café/restaurant (Mon–Sat 9am–10pm, Sun 9am–2pm) and an art centre that stages excellent exhibitions of contemporary art – home-grown and international – and

The Forn des Teatre

has a permanent display of the work of Catalan painter Hermen Anglada Camarasa (1872–1959), who lived in Pollença. This was the first modern hotel in Mallorca, built in 1903 by Lluís Doménech i Muntaner. After a chequered history it was acquired in 1987 by La Caixa, a savings bank that does a lot for the arts in Catalunya and the Balearic Islands.

Across from the Gran Hotel is a small bakery and café, the **Forn des Teatre**, whose graceful facade graces many a postcard. Down the street, on Plaça Mercat, stand the two gently undulating *Moderniste* buildings that comprise **Can Casayas**. The bakery got its name from the neighbouring **Teatre Principal**, a grand edifice that re-opened in 2007 after extensive renovation work and stages plays, operas and concerts *(see page 92)*. Follow the road past the theatre and you reach **Via Roma**, an avenue called La Rambla, after Barcelona's promenade, but despite shady plane trees and flower stalls it has neither the architecture nor the buzz of its namesake.

Barrí Sant Miquel

Turn right from Plaça Major, instead of descending the steps, and you will be in Carrer Sant Miquel, a busy pedes-trianised shopping street, where the **Museu d'Art Espanyol**

Contemporani (Mon–Fri 10am–6.30pm, Sat 10.30am–2pm; free) is located. This striking 18th-century building, with marble staircases and good stained glass, houses an exceptional collection belonging to the wealthy March banking family. The 70-strong permanent collection includes works by Picasso, Miró, Dalí, Tàpies and Juan Gris. Next door to the museum, the Banco March is open for business in a marble-pillared, wood-panelled setting.

Heading north up the street you will come to the church of **Sant Miquel** (Mon–Sat 8am–1.30pm, 5–7.30pm, Sun 10am–1pm, 6–7.30pm), where the first Mass after the Christian reconquest was celebrated. This ancient church is the religious heart of the neighbourhood, a solid building with a fine baroque altarpiece. A little further on is the deconsecrated church of **Sant Antoniet** (Mon–Fri 10.30am–1.30pm, 5–8.30pm, Sat 10.30am–1.30pm; free), whose pretty courtyard plays host to a variety of temporary art exhibitions, and

The March Dynasty

The Fundació March was set up by the extremely wealthy March banking dynasty in 1955 as a philanthropic institution to promote science and culture. You will see branches of the Banca March all over the Balearic Islands, and notice their name appended to numerous cultural ventures. As well as the two major museums mentioned here, there is an extensive library and archive in the Palau March, also open to the public, and concerts are held there in summer. The foundation also funds an annual programme of 20th-century classical music at Palma's Auditorio and summer concerts in the Jardins March in Cala Ratjada (see page 94), where there is some splendid modern sculpture. Annual prizes for literary criticism and short novels are also awarded by a dynasty that obviously believes in putting a lot back into the community on which its wealth was founded.

Shopping at the market

the walls and pavement outside have become an informal gallery space for local amateur artists.

Round the corner, on the right, is the **Mercat de l'Olivar** (daily), the city's largest fish, meat and produce market. A very short distance further along Carrer Caputxins is the Plaça d'Espanya, where you will find the new Estació Intermodal, the combined rail, metro and bus station.

Passeig des Born to the Waterfront

If you go west instead of north from Plaça Weyler, along traffic-filled Carrer Unió, you come to Plaça Rei Joan Carles I. Ahead is the busy shopping street, Avinguda Jaume III; to your left, the leafy **Passeig des Born**. The broad central avenue, lined with benches and guarded at either end by stone sphinxes, runs down to **Plaça de la Reina**, with a large central fountain. At No. 27, the elegant 18th-century **Palau Solleric** (Tue–Sat 10am–2pm, 5–9pm, Sun 10am–1pm) houses a cultural foundation, hosts contemporary art exhibitions and has a café and bookshop and a tourist information desk.

To the left of Plaça de la Reina (past the tourist office, *see page 130*) steps lead up to the cathedral, where we began. Hugging the old city walls is **S'Hort del Rei**, a lovely Arabic-style garden, with fountains and pools, which makes a pleasant distraction from city traffic. Miró's beloved **Personatge** sculpture ('The Egg') stands on the corner nearest the *plaça*. Facing it is the new, cool and minimalist café that is part of the Palau March *(see page 31)*. Parallel to S'Hort del Rei, a much-needed car park has been constructed beneath a stretch of the Avinguda Antoni Maura. Below the city walls, on the southern side, the attractively landscaped **Parc de la Mar** forms a barrier against the coastal motorway, the **Passeig Marítim**. The park has an artificial lake and modern sculpture, including works by Miró, and is the venue for free open-air concerts on summer evenings, as is Ses Voltes, lying directly beneath the Cathedral walls.

A right turn here leads to the turreted **Sa Llotja** in the square of the same name. Designed in the 15th century by Guillem Sagrera (after whom this stretch of the Passeig Marítim is named), it was once the merchants' stock exchange, and is one of Spain's finest civic Gothic buildings, with slim columns twisting through a light and airy interior to the vaulted roof. It is used for art exhibitions but is currently undergoing extensive renovation work. Nearby **Plaça Drassana** is a pleasant if somewhat shabby neighbourhood square. Here, the 17th-century **Consolat de Mar**, the former maritime law court is also being renovated. The two buildings are linked by the Porta del Mar, one of the old city gates. The maze of narrow streets between Plaça de Sa Llotja and Plaça de la

Miró's Personatge sculpture

Reina form Palma's lively restaurant and nightlife area *(see pages 94 and 107)*.

Cross the road at the nearest traffic lights to explore Palma's harbour and waterfront, in all its diversity. There are fishermen mending their nets (although the fishing fleet is not what it was), smart yachts around the **Real Club Náutic**, a tiny fishermen's chapel, Sant Elm, opportunities to take trips around the harbour, and, at the western end, the ferry passenger terminal. En route, several pleasant cafés and restaurants overlook the port, while cyclists, runners and roller-bladers whizz past on a designated track. The harbour front is planted with palms, hibiscus and oleander, but there is no ignoring the fact that six lanes of traffic are roaring past on the other side. Despite this, it is very pleasant on a summer evening, when the sun is setting over the water and there's a great view of the illuminated cathedral.

Almost opposite the Real Club Náutic is the prestigious **Es Baluard Museu d'Art Modern i Contemporani** (mid-Jun–Sept: Tue–Sun 10am–10pm; Oct–mid-Jun: Tue–Fri 10am–8pm; charge), housed in a stunning white structure built into the city fortifications in Plaça Porta de Santa Catalina. Displays include work by Picasso, Miró and Tàpies as well as Mallorcan artists Miquel Barceló and Juli Ramis. The views of the port and the city from the museum's rooftop and terrace are impressive. Classical music recitals are held in the museum on some evenings.

Out-of-Town Attractions

Further west are three more places worth mentioning. The **Poble Espanyol** (Apr–Oct: daily 9am–7pm; Nov–Mar: 9am–6pm; charge), a walled town of replica architectural treasures from across Spain, is kitsch but entertaining. The buildings house shops, craft studios, bars and cafés. It is reached by bus No. 46 from the Plaça d'Espanya or Plaça

Rei Joan Carles I, or by the Turistbus *(see page 130)*.

Just south of the Poble Espanyol, perched on a hilltop, is **Castell de Bellver** (Apr–Sept Mon–Sat 8.30am–8.30pm, Sun 10am–7pm; Oct–Mar 8.30am–7pm, Sun 10am–5pm; charge), reached on bus No. 50 from Plaça d'Espanya or the Turistbus. A magnificent example of Gothic military architecture, the castle has commanded the approaches to the city since the 14th century. From the battlements the view of the city and the bay is quite stunning. Inside, the small **Museu d'Història de la Ciutat** (closed Sunday) traces the history and archaeology of the area.

Moorish-style arches at the Poble Espanyol

The best of the three is the **Fundació Pilar i Joan Miró** (mid-May–mid-Sept: Tue–Sat 10am–7pm; mid-Sept–mid-May till 6pm; Sun 10am–3pm all year; charge) in Carrer Joan de Saridakis in the suburb of Cala Major. Bus No. 3 or 46 from the Plaça d'Espanya or Plaça Rei Joan Carles will take you right to the door, but a taxi from the centre is not expensive. The Catalan artist and his Mallorcan wife lived on the island from 1956 until his death in 1983, and the foundation, in a streamlined white building designed by Rafael Moneo and surrounded by gardens and ponds, displays a fine selection of his work.

THE WESTERN CORNER

When tourism hit Mallorca, the Bay of Palma, with two magnificent sweeps of white sand almost 30km (18 miles) long, was irresistible, and the resorts that mushroomed along here in the 1960s and 1970s gave the island a name for cheap and cheerful holidays. The picture soon turned decidedly tacky, dominated by down-market tourism and high-rise hotels.

To the west of the bay, things start to improve after Camp de Mar, where the coast road winds through forest to Port d'Andratx. After a detour to Sant Elm, at the island's southwestern tip, there is a beautiful winding coast road to the village of Banyalbufar. Then head inland via the La Granja estate and La Reserva Puig de Galatzó, after which you can complete the circle back to Palma, or carry on up the picturesque west coast. For the southern end of the bay, *see page 81).*

West of the Bay

You can either take the **Via Cintura** (ring road), which becomes the MA-1 motorway at Porto Pi, or the coast road. Either way, you will see a turn off to **Cala Major** (where the Spanish royal family have their summer home). The coast road runs through the resorts of **Sant Agustí**, with a small yacht harbour, and crowded **Ses Illetes**, to a rocky stretch of coast and the exclusive **Bendinat** and **Portals Nous**. Here, apartment cluster on the slopes and a glamorous marina, **Puerto Portals**, has been carved out of the cliffs. All very classy.

Nemo Submarine

For an underwater adventure, take a 50-minute trip on the Nemo Submarine from Magaluf. There's lots of underwater life to see and it's very comfortable and well organised, if a bit expensive. Tours every hour, Mar–Oct: 9am–5pm; advance booking necessary, tel: 971 130 244, or go to Carrer Galeón 2, Magaluf.

Portals Vells

Sandy beaches start again at the resorts of **Costa d'En Blanes** – where the popular dolphinarium, **Marineland** *(see page 95)*, is situated – and **Palma Nova**. The latter blends almost imperceptibly into big, brash **Magaluf**. The wide, sandy beach is a solid block of bronzing bodies by day; the town centre an equally solid stretch of drinkers by night. This is tourism overkill: vast bars and discos, restaurants offering frankfurters, curry and all-day English breakfasts, wide-screen televised football, and some of the trashiest shops imaginable.

A road lined by pines runs south to the pretty cove of **Portals Vells**, which has somehow escaped much development. In the cliffs are huge caverns dating from Roman times, enlarged over the centuries. Boats make the short excursion from the pier at Magaluf, so it's not always peaceful. Not far south of Portals Vells, you can walk to the tranquil cove of **Cala Figuera** (one of three coves on the island with this name), but the end of the peninsula is a military zone.

Port d'Andratx and Sant Elm

Pick up the main road (which is motorway as far as Peguera) but turn off at Camp de Mar where a scenic road twists through pine forest to **Port d'Andratx**. More yachts than fishing boats bob on the calm waters of the bay these days. The old harbour area still looks traditional but a string of chic restaurants and shops lines it, and villas and apartments climb the slopes across the water. But the lack of a sandy beach has kept the big hotels and package tours away and Port d'Andratx feels relaxed.

The quiet inland town of Andratx plays host to the impressive **Centro Cultural Andratx** (Tue–Fri 10.30am–7pm, Sat–Sun 10.30am–4pm; admission fee), established by a Danish couple, which stages contemporary art exhibitions and runs artists' workshops. From here you could make a detour to **Sant Elm**, the island's westernmost point, a former fishing vil-

Port d'Andratx

lage that has retained its identity, though sailors, surfers
and divers have known about
it for a long time. Offshore,
the nature-reserve island of
Sa Dragonera, can be visited by boat in the summer.

Up the Scenic Coast

From Andratx the C710 runs
across the southern reaches
of the Serra de Tramuntana,
around numerous hairpin
bends to the coast, where it

View up the coast from
Mirador de Ricardo Roca

winds along the cliff tops. To the right are terraces planted
with fruit trees and olives and some delightful little villages. Along the road stands a succession of *miradors*,
lookout points with commanding views of the entire coast,
still crowned with ancient watchtowers from which look-
outs once scanned the sea for pirate ships. The **Mirador**
de Ricardo Roca has fantastic views of the coast, and a
huge restaurant in which to sit and enjoy them.

   Estellencs, some 4km (2½ miles) on, is an ancient village,
set amid orange groves on the slopes of Puig de Galatzó
(1,026m/3,360ft). From the town you can walk or drive
down a track to a little fishing cove. Another 5km (3 miles)
further on, one of the finest views of the coast can be had
from the 16th-century tower of the **Mirador de Ses Ànimes**.
The next town, **Banyalbufar**, is a pretty place with Moorish
origins. The Arabic name means 'vineyard by the sea', and
it is still famous for its terraced hillsides, a popular haunt for
artists. There are a couple of pleasant hotels, several restaurants, and a lane twists down to a rocky cove whose crystal-
clear water is ideal for diving.

Music and folk dancing at
La Granja

La Granja

North of Banyalbufar, the road turns inland, in the direction of **Esporles**, close to which you'll find the estate of **La Granja** (May–Oct: daily 10am–7pm; Nov–Apr: 10am–6pm; www.lagranja. net; charge). It's a bit of a theme park, but well worth a visit. In Roman times the estate was renowned for the purity of its water, and there are still numerous fountains in the leafy gardens. The interior of the house is magnificent and gives a good idea of how the landed classes once lived. The chapel and the torture chamber speak for themselves. The donkeys, pigs, wild goats and sheep in the grounds are usually a hit with children. There are tastings of fig bread and local cheese and sausages, and on Wednesday and Friday from 3.30–5pm there are handicraft demonstrations and performances of regional music, folk dancing and dressage.

From here, you can return to Palma on the PM104, continue up the west coast, or take the minor road to Puigpunyent to visit **La Reserva Puig de Galatzó** (Jun–Aug: daily 10am–7pm; Sept–May: 10am–6.30pm; last admittance 2 hours before closing; charge). Some 3km (2 miles) of paths run past waterfalls and caves through protected land, rich in bird and animal life, on the lush slopes of Galatzó, known as the mystical mountain because of its magnetic properties. The paths are fairly easy, although you need sensible shoes. If you want something more adventurous you can try abseiling, climbing, mountain biking and crossing suspension bridges – although these so-called 'Adventure Trails' are quite expensive.

THE WEST COAST

This is one of the most dramatic and beautiful routes in Mallorca. It's hard to pick a highlight as there are so many, from Valldemossa, where George Sand and Frédéric Chopin once stayed, to the lovely hilltop village of Deià, once home to poet Robert Graves, the cliff-top mansion of the Habsburg Archduke Ludwig, and the agreeable town of Sóller.

Whether you are continuing a route round the coast on the C710 or coming direct from Palma on the PM111, a good, straightish road, running through groves of olives and almonds, your first stop will be at Valldemossa. As you approach, the incline becomes steeper and the village and monastery suddenly appear, like a fairytale settlement.

La Real Cartuja de Valldemossa

Although **Valldemossa** was the birthplace of Mallorca's only home-grown saint, Catalina Tomás *(see below)*, it was the visit, in the winter of 1838–39, of French writer George Sand – Armandine Dupin-Dudevant – and her lover,

Catalina Tomás

Santa Catalina is Mallorca's very own saint. She was born in Valldemossa in 1531 in a house at Carrer Rectoría 5, behind the church, which is now a shrine. There is another, smaller shrine with a fountain and ferns in Carrer de la Beatà, a quiet corner where caged birds sing. Almost every house has a tiled picture outside, depicting scenes from the saint's life and asking her blessing: 'Santa Catalina Tomás Pregau Per Nosaltres'. She was a farmer's daughter, marked out as special when still a child, and taken to Palma by a sympathetic patron, where she worked as a servant in a wealthy household before entering the convent of Santa Magdalena and taking her vows.

Frédéric Chopin, that really put the town on the map. They don't seem to have been very happy here; Chopin was unwell, the weather was miserable, and the villagers disapproved of Sand's habit of wearing men's clothes and smoking cigars. She disparaged the local people in her book, *A Winter in Majorca*, calling them 'barbarians and thieves', although she thought Mallorca 'the most beautiful place I have ever lived'.

Nowadays, coach loads of visitors disturb the peace of the little hilltop town as they come to see the couple's lodgings in the former Carthusian monastery, **La Real Cartuja de Valldemossa** (Mar–Oct Mon–Sat 9.30am–6pm, Sun 10am–1pm; Nov–Feb: 10.30am–4.30pm; charge). The monastery was founded in 1399, but when the monks were expelled in 1835 some of their cells were sold as apartments – although the 'cells' were three-room suites with private gardens. Those rented by Sand and Chopin are now a museum, which displays manuscripts, Chopin's death mask and his piano. You can also visit the massive church, the pharmacy, with a beautiful collection of 18th-century ceramic jars, the library and the Prior's Cell, complete with a life-size model of a prior. There is an interesting **Museu Municipal** here, too, with documents relating to the Archduke Lud-

Valldemossa monastery

wig *(see page 50)*; and an **art gallery** displaying paintings by Joan Miró, Max Ernst and Antoni Saura as well as Mallorcan landscapes.

The adjoining 16th-century palace, the **Palau del Rei Sanxo** (hours as for La Cartuja; combined ticket), was constructed on the site of one Jaume II built for his son, Sanxo, and is entered through a tranquil, plant-filled courtyard. Piano recitals of Chopin's music are held throughout the day.

Chopin's death mask, amongst memorabilia at the monastery

Around the Town

Outside the monastery is a cobbled *plaça* shaded with lime trees – *tilos* – which give the square its name. The streets around it, and those leading to the 13th-century church of Sant Bartomeu, dedicated to Santa Catalina, are bright with potted plants, and the steepest, most slippery parts are covered with strips of carpet to prevent trippers tripping up.

The main street in the lower town, where there are adequate car parks, is lined with cafés and restaurants and some interesting little shops, selling jewellery and clothes made of cool, natural fibres. One of the nicest bars (just back from the main street, on Carrer Blanquera) serves delicious *horchata (see page 103)*, fresh juice and good coffee and hot chocolate, along with *cocas de patata*, the sugar-dusted, potato-shaped buns, tasting not unlike *ensaimadas*, that are a local speciality.

On the edge of town, at Avda Palma 6, is the **Centro Cultural Costa Nord** (daily 9am–5pm; tel: 971 612 425 for de-

Picturesque Port de Valldemossa

tails), founded by Michael Douglas, who has had a home nearby for many years, and who narrates the commentary to a virtual reality tour of the region. There is also a restaurant here and the centre organises guided excursions.

In the other direction, a few metres along the road towards Banyalbufar, a vertiginous road leads 6km (4 miles) down to the tiny **Port de Valldemossa** where there's a small gravel beach and crystal-clear water. On summer weekends, however, the narrow road and the limited parking area become uncomfortably busy.

Son Marroig

The coastal C710 continues north, with stunning sea views to the left, and groves of ancient, gnarled olive trees among huge boulders to the right. After about 6km (4 miles), a track signposted simply **Miramar** leads to the ruins of a monastery founded by Ramon Lull. Only part of the cloister remains, but there is also a chapel and a museum with artefacts collected by Archduke Ludwig *(see below)*, including a model of his beloved steam-driven yacht, *Nixe*. A short way further on, a sign points to **Son Marroig** (Mon–Sat 9am–8pm; till sunset in winter; charge), a manor house that belonged to the Austrian Archduke Ludwig Salvator of Habsburg-Lorraine and Bourbon, who had a life-long love affair with the Balearics and their people. Born in Florence in 1847, he renounced courtly life in Vienna and spent years travelling the world on scientific explorations, returning often to the estate he bought in 1870 on this beautiful stretch of coast. Several rooms can be visited, filled with paintings, photos and ceramics. In the gardens, there's a wonderful view from a cliff-edge white temple of Carrara marble.

Hundreds of metres below the house is **Na Foradada**, a rocky promontory, pierced by a remarkable 18-m (60-ft) wide natural window. If you visit the house, ask for permission to make the half-hour walk down to the sea and the landing stage where the Archduke used to anchor the *Nixe*. The café near the car park is a wonderful place from which to watch the sunset. (For details of concerts at Son Marroig during the Deià International Music Festival, *see page 94*.)

Deià

Set on the slopes of the 1,062-m (3,484-ft) Teix massif, **Deià** ◀ ⓫ is a delight, a pretty town of honey-coloured stone that has

The Teix massif forms a dramatic backdrop to pretty little Deià

attracted artists, writers and assorted expatriates ever since the Archduke Ludwig first came here. He was followed by the Catalan poet and painter Santiago Rusinyol, at the turn of the 20th century, later by writer Anaïs Nin (1903–77) and the American archaeologist William Waldren. But it is Robert Graves, the poet and author of *I, Claudius* and the autobiographical *Goodbye to All That*, who came here with American writer Laura Riding in 1929, who is most closely associated with the place. Graves loved Deià and fiercely defended the northwest coast against commercial exploitation. It was largely due to his efforts that the area was designated a protected zone. His home, **Ca N'Alluny** (Mon–Fri 10am–4pm, Sat 10am–2pm; charge) on the Carretera Deià–Sóller, has been restored and opened as a museum. The house and garden are delightful, and retain much of their original character as well as exhibiting the writer's effects.

You must leave your car on the main street, which is lined with restaurants, galleries and shops selling attractive summer clothes. Narrow, winding streets lead to the top of the village and the little church of **Sant Joan Bautista**. Beside it is a small cemetery overlooking the Mediterranean; a simple cement slab bears the inscription 'Robert Graves, Poeta, 1895–1985'.

Deià is extremely popular, and many chic well-heeled people have holiday homes here. Besides a luxury hotel, La Residencia, there are several less expensive alternatives *(see pages 135–6)*, and the best selection of restaurants on the coast *(see page 109)*.

Cala de Deià

Just past the village, a twisting 2-km (1-mile) drive takes you down to **Cala de Deià**, a tiny cove with a rocky beach, where ramps emerge from boathouses set into the cliffs. The water is clear, buoyant and safe and there are

Cala de Deià

two reasonable beach cafés. Don't imagine you've found a secluded beach, though. Regular visitors know it well and it can get very busy at weekends. You can walk to the beach, too, either by following steps near the vehicle access road, or by walking down steep Carrer Bauza at the Valldemossa end of the village, following the course of a stream past pretty gardens till the village peters out and the path continues through groves of lemons and olives; it takes about 35 minutes in all.

Sóller and its Port

From Deià, the coast road, lined with groves of oranges, lemons and almonds as well as olives, descends into the broad valley of Sóller. The scenery is lovely and the town of **Sóller** itself is a little gem, a busy, prosperous place that claims, like several others, to have been the birthplace of Columbus. It is full of well-preserved 18th- and 19th-century mansions, and the main square, **Plaça Sa Constitució**, with numerous cafés, is a good place to sit and absorb the town's character. Like the main street, the Gran Via, it has *Moderniste* (Catalan Art Nouveau) flourishes, a legacy of early 20th-century expansion. The church of **Sant Bartomeu** (Mon–Thur 11am–1.15pm, 3–5.15pm, Fri–Sat 11am–1.15pm; free) is a huge building with a baroque interior and attractive stained-glass windows. Its *Moderniste* exterior, like that of the Banco Central Hispano on the opposite corner, was designed by a pupil of Antoni Gaudí.

The station at the top of the town is another splendid *Moderniste* building. You can make an old-fashioned journey on a little wooden train that has been running from here to Palma and back on a narrow-gauge railway since 1912 (journey time about an hour).

The station has another attraction, too: the Sala Miró (daily 10.30am–6.30pm; free), hung with drawings and lithographs by the artist; and a second gallery *(same hours)* that displays some 50 ceramic pieces by Picasso.

Tipico de Sóller

Sóller is a good place to try freshly squeezed orange juice *(zumo de naranja)*, as the orange groves around the town are reputed to produce the very best juice oranges. You could also sample the local orange liqueur, called Angel d'Or, which is used to flavour some of the cakes found on menus and in Sóller's many tempting cake shops.

Outside the station you can get information on hiking *(senderisme)* from the tourist office (tel: 971 633 042), housed in an old train carriage. Here, too, you can catch the **Orange Tram** that rattles on a scenic, 20-minute journey to **Port de Sóller** (departs every half hour 7am–8.25pm; tickets sold on board), stopping en route where requested. This is a good old-fashioned little resort, with a fine harbour, and it has gained a few smart restaurants and bars in recent years. You can hire canoes, take sailing or windsurfing lessons or make boat trips around the bay or further afield to Sa Calobra and Na Foradada (*see page 85*).

Two Gardens

Just outside town, on the ring road, is the **Museu Balear de Ciències Naturales i Jardí Botànic** (Tue–Sat 10am–6pm, Sun 10am–2pm; charge). The museum is of no great interest but the grounds contain a collection of aromatic herbs and plants

Sóller's Orange Tram

from all over the Balearic Islands, a vegetable garden and a 'peace garden'.

The road from Sóller to Palma, with numerous hairpin bends and the 496-m (1,627-ft) **Coll de Sóller** pass to negotiate, was believed to be so daunting that it impeded the development of the area. Despite the protests of some environmentalists, a tunnel was constructed under the mountains, reducing travel time to Palma to about half an hour (toll currently €5).

At the southern exit from the tunnel (on the left) are the **Jardins d'Alfàbia** (Apr–Oct: Mon–Sat 9.30am–6.30pm; Nov–Mar: Mon–Fri 9.30am–5.30pm, Sat 9.30am–1pm; charge), a baronial mansion with wonderful gardens, that

13

was once the country estate of a Moorish *vizier* of Palma. The cisterns, fountains and irrigation channels are a bit neglected, but the flowing water and shaded walks, with turkeys pecking under fig trees, and birds singing among exotic plants, are appealing. The house is full of treasures: look out for the huge, 14th-century oak chair in the print room, regarded as the most important antique in Mallorca. There's also an excellent restaurant, Ses Porxeres, next door *(see page 110).* (If you want to visit the gardens and don't have transport, check with the information office at Palma bus station for bus details.)

From Bunyola to the Castle

A few kilometres past the gardens a left-hand turn points to **Bunyola**, a peaceful little place that produces excellent olive oil and a bright green herbal liqueur called Palo Tunel. The village church and the town hall both stand on the main square, Sa Plaça, which is shaded by leafy plane trees. It's a lovely drive from here to the tiny village of **Orient**, which has a hotel and several restaurants and is a favourite base for hikers. The **Castell d'Alaró**, a ruined fortress built by Jaume I, crowns a massive crag 822m (2,700ft) high.

You can walk up from Orient if you have lots of energy, strong shoes and a supply of drinking water, or drive most of the way to the summit up narrow, tortuous lanes, starting a little north of nearby **Alaró**. The tracks get progressively rougher, however, and the final stretch is only suitable for 4-wheel-drive vehicles. Park before this section begins, at the Bar Es Pouet, and look for a sign saying 'Castell a Peu' (To the castle on foot). That leaves a 30- to 40-minute climb to do, not advisable in the heat of summer. The views from the top are spectacular. There is a small restaurant and simple accommodation, which must be booked in advance (tel: 971 182 112).

Fornalutx – so pretty it's been designated a national monument

The Heart of the Tramuntana

If you go in the opposite direction from Sóller, towards Pollença, there are more magnificent views as the road cuts through the heart of the Serra de Tramuntana, over the pass of **Puig Major**, Mallorca's highest mountain at 1,445m/4,741ft.

Fornalutx is an exquisite little town of warm stone buildings that has been designated a national monument – which naturally means that it draws in a lot of visitors, but also means building regulations are stringent. Set against the backdrop of the Tramuntana range, its steep cobbled streets are lined with cacti and palm trees. A high number of the well-restored medieval properties belong to foreigners, attracted by the region's beauty. The town is set among ancient terraces of citrus fruits and gnarled olive trees, marked out with dry-stone walls. Paths run through them to pretty little **Biniaraix**, which is also only a half-hour walk down narrow lanes, signposted from the centre of Sóller.

A short distance past Fornalutx on the C710, the **Mirador de Ses Barques** has a restaurant where you can stop for a drink while enjoying views of the coast and Port de Sóller. The route then winds past the reservoirs of Panta de Cúber and Panta de Gorg-Blau, connected by a narrow canal. Near the latter, a little road leads down to the coast. Its name, **Sa Calobra** (The Snake), is an apt one for the 12km (8 miles) of hairpin bends that loop down to sea level. The views are stunning and the road is an adventure in itself, but try to come fairly early in the morning to avoid the streams of tourist coaches.

Park where you can when the road reaches sea level and walk a short distance towards the deep gorge of **Torrent de Pareis**. Tunnels burrow through the rock to the riverbed where the gorge widens into a huge natural theatre. The idyllic little bay, **Cala de Sa Calobra**, has a couple of restaurants and bars and a pebbly beach, but they get crowded in summer.

Cala de Sa Calobra is idyllic

Monestir de Lluc

Around 10km (6 miles) further along the road to Pollença is the major pilgrimage site in Mallorca, the **Monestir de Lluc** (daily 10am–6.30pm, free; museum 10am–1.30pm and 2.30–5.30pm, charge). Located in a valley near Puig des Castellot, the massive building mainly dates from the 18th century, but pilgrims have been coming here since the 13th century to pray to a dark-stone statue of the Madonna and Child, La Moreneta. According to

The Monestir de Lluc attracts tourists and pilgrims

legend, it was discovered by an Arab boy called Lluc, whose family had converted to Christianity. He took the statue to the church of Sant Pere in the tiny village of Escorça nearby, but it kept returning to the place where he had found it, so it was finally allowed to stay and a chapel was built to house it.

People still come to venerate La Moreneta, but many also come to have lunch and admire the views, for the monastery has a restaurant, bar and barbecue area. It also offers inexpensive accommodation (tel: 971 871 525); the rooms are fairly basic, but staying here allows you to appreciate the peace of the monastery after the tour groups have gone home. Attend Mass in the church (daily 11am) for the experience of hearing the Lluc boys' choir, the **Coro Blavets** (Blue Ones), named after the colour of their cassocks. If you are staying overnight you may be able to hear the choir at 6.45pm (check when booking accommodation).

THE NORTH AND NORTHEAST

The north is a region of great variety. It encompasses the rugged Cap de Formentor, the sandy coves of Sant Vicenç, two attractive towns – Pollença and Alcúdia – the resort of Port de Pollença and the huge, curved Badia d'Alcúdia, lined with resorts and facilities. Parallel to the bay is a complete contrast in the wetlands of the Parc Natural de S'Albufera

From Palma, it's a fast drive up the MA13 motorway to the MA220 turning to Pollença. If continuing the previous route, the road from Lluc curves through holm oak forests before descending to the Vall de Son Marc and Pollença.

Pollença

18 **Pollença** has a long history. The Romans established a settlement here after they moved inland from Alcúdia/Pollentia *(see page 66)*, and the stone bridge to the north of the town centre is Roman in origin. The Catalan community was

---

Puig de Santa Maria

Just outside Pollença on the Palma road is a path up to the **Santuari del Puig**, the ruined convent on 333-m (1,092-ft) **Puig de Santa Maria**. The first half of the 4-km (2-mile) trail can be done by car, the latter part on foot. The dry-stone walls *(margers)* along the last section are a good demonstration of an ancient skill that is now dying out. The views from the top, stretching as far as the Serra de Tramuntana, Cap de Formentor, the plain of Sa Pobla and the bays of Alcúdia and Pollença, are superb. The Gothic convent was founded in the 14th century and soon became one of the most sacred buildings on the island. Accommodation is available and there are self-catering facilities, a bar and a restaurant (prior notice needed for accommodation, tel: 971 184 132).

founded in 1236 after the Moors were expelled. Present-day Pollença was first shown on a map in 1789; it was a prosperous town, the property of the Order of the Knights of St John until 1802, and able to support the numerous impressive churches still standing.

The cockerel on the fountain is a symbol of Pollença

Pollença is a lively place, especially on summer evenings when it fills with visitors; the comings and goings in the **Plaça Major** provide free entertainment for people sipping cool drinks outside one of several cafés and restaurants. The *plaça* also comes into its own on Sunday morning, when local people shop for fresh produce in the market, then drink coffee outside the Café Espanyol after attending Mass in the parochial church, **La Mare de Déu des Àngels**.

The Carrer de Monte-Sion leading off the square towards the Jesuit church of the same name (under renovation), has some great little shops and a number of restaurants. Good ceramics can be found in Monte-Sion Cerámica, which has a display of old decorated tiles – unfortunately not for sale. Nearby is little Plazuela de la Almoina; the fountain has a cockerel on top, the symbol of the town. In Carrer Roca the **Fundació i Casa Museu Dionís Bennassar** (Jul–Sept: Tue–Sat 10.30am–1.30pm, 6–8.30pm, Sun 10.30am–1.30pm; Oct–Jun: Tue–Sun 10.30am–1.30pm; charge) displays the work and personal possessions of this local artist (1904–67) in his family home.

From the parish church in the *plaça* (or from the Ajuntament, off to the left), the **Via Crucis** (Way of the Cross), a flight of 365 steps lined with cypress trees, leads to **El Calvari**. This little chapel has been given a rhyming name – **La Mare de Déu del Peu de la Creu** (Mother of God at the Foot of the Cross) – after a 14th-century sculpture inside showing Mary at the feet of Christ.

Back in town, the deconsecrated Dominican convent and church of **Sant Domingo** (church, cloister and museum May–Sept: Tue–Fri 10.30am–1pm, 5.30–11pm, Sat–Sun 11am–1pm; Oct–Apr: 10.30am–1pm only; charge for museum) is now devoted to culture rather than worship. Exhibitions of installation art are staged in the nave of the great 17th-century church in summer, and the cloisters are the venue for a classical music festival in July and August *(see page 94)*, when an international line up of orchestras and soloists performs. Pollença's **Museu Municipal** is also housed inside the monastery in a large, light space. Somewhat eclectic, it includes changing exhibitions of contemporary paintings and sculpture, a permanent collection of Gothic art, some early 20th-century paintings and a few archaeological finds.

Pollença's Via Crucis

Outside the convent, the **Jardins Joan March Severa**, built around a watchtower, have an interesting collection of Balearic plants. Carrer Roser Vell leads off to the left; at its far end you will see the plain facade of the little 14th-century oratory of **Roser Vell** (Apr–Oct: Mon–Fri 5–7pm; Nov–Mar: 3–5pm; free).

Boats moored in Port de Pollença

Cala Sant Vicenç and Port de Pollença

About 3km (2 miles) along the PM220 from Pollença to its port is the turning to **Cala Sant Vicenç**, a glossy resort built around three gorgeous sandy coves with brilliant blue water, excellent for swimming and snorkelling – although strong winds can get up quite quickly. The setting, framed by the craggy Serra de Comayaques and El Morral mountains, is spectacular; try to ignore the modern hotel on the headland.

A couple more kilometres along the main road brings you to **Port de Pollença**. Set on the wide curve of a bay, with the marina in the centre, it has been popular with English visitors for many years and retains a distinctive atmosphere. However, it is a resort with a split personality. To the north of the marina the promenade has a plethora of restaurants, some with tables set on the beach, and a couple of stylish hotels. These give way to old, one-storey houses and wooden jetties, where the branches of trees almost reach the water.

Hermen Camarasa

On the promenade north of the marina you may notice a memorial bust of Hermen Anglada Camarasa (1872–1959), the Catalan *Moderniste* painter after whom this stretch is named. He lived and worked in Pollença for many years. A collection of his work can be seen in the Gran Hotel in Palma (see pages 35–6).

To the south of the marina, however, the palm-shaded promenade that parallels the lovely, long sweep of sandy beach is lined wall-to-wall with cheap and cheerful tripper shops and fast-food joints. The narrow streets behind the promenade are nicer. There's a lot to do, however: sailing and scuba lessons are on offer, and there are boat trips to Formentor and Cala Sant Vicenç.

Cap de Formentor

Continuing round the bay to the southeast, towards Alcúdia, the commercial zone ends abruptly and the beach becomes a narrow strip, popular with windsurfers, with an expanse of lonely wetlands on the other side.

But before heading in this direction, make a trip to the island's northernmost point, **Cap de Formentor**, the narrow headland on the north side of the Badia de Pollença. With sheer cliffs and idyllic sandy beaches, the rocky peninsula, surrounded by clear turquoise waters, is simply spectacular. The best place to appreciate the extraordinary landscape is the **Mirador des Colomer**, about 5km (3 miles) from Port de Pollença, where there is a specially designed walkway. Some tour buses don't go any further than this, which is a blessing for motorists, as the twisting road is a challenging one, demanding much concentration, and can get swamped with traffic in summer.

The pretty, pine-shaded beach (signposted Platja de Formentor on the right-hand side), is a favourite spot for a picnic and offers splendid views across the bay – similar to those you would get from the exclusive Hotel Formentor, whose manicured gardens are visible from the beach. The hotel was built in 1928 by an Argentinian architect, Adam Diehl, and quickly became popular with a fashionable set which, over the next few decades, included the Duke of Windsor and Mrs Simpson, Sir Winston Churchill and the Rainiers of Monaco, and is still the haunt of the rich and famous.

From the beach turn-off it's about another 12km (8 miles) to the lighthouse on the tip. Just before you enter the tunnel that leads through the Fumat mountain, there's a great view of the sparkling waters of **Cala Figuera** far below, one of the most unspoilt beaches on the island. You may prefer to turn off down the single-track path to the tiny cove rather than continuing to the lighthouse. If you do carry on to the end, you'll find that the tiny car park can get crowded.

Appreciating the rugged cape scenery at Mirador des Colomer

Alcúdia

Retrace your steps now past Port de Pollença to the ancient, walled town of **Alcúdia**. There were Phoenician and Greek settlements here before the Romans founded their city in 123BC, and called it Pollentia (Power). They stayed for about five centuries before moving inland to present-day Pollença. The Vandals sacked it, the Moors rebuilt it – Al Kudia (means 'on the hill') – and the conquering Spaniards fortified it in the 13th century. The massive walls and gates now standing are later imitations, but still impressive. Today, it's a nice, unpretentious little place, with some excellent Renaissance facades, good cafés and restaurants on the central **Plaça Constitució**, and a lively Sunday market, held just outside the walls.

The sturdy neo-Gothic church of **Sant Jaume** and adjoining **Museu Parroquial** form the southern bastion in the walls

Alfresco dining in Alcúdia

(currently closed to the public). Opposite the church, in a small, 14th-century building, is the **Museo Monogràfic de Pollentia** (Tue–Fri 10am–4pm, Sat–Sun 10am–2pm; combined entrance ticket with Ciutat Romana). It has an extensive collection of Roman finds, including ceramics, glassware, tools and surgical instruments. You can pick up a free leaflet

Alcúdia's city wall

here describing points of interest in the Roman city. The remains of that city, the **Ciutat Romana del Pollentia** (hours as above), excavated in the 1950s by members of a dig organised by American archaeologist William Bryant, stand outside the walls (there's a large car park and a bus from Palma stops nearby). The area includes remnants of two buildings, and gives a good idea of the town's layout. The **Teatre Romà**, outside the city proper, on the road to the port, is impressive and the acoustics (which are tested by many visitors) are great.

Port d'Alcúdia and the Bay

Port d'Alcúdia (from where you can get a ferry to Menorca) has evolved from a small fishing harbour into an all-purpose port for commercial, naval and pleasure craft and the largest resort on the north coast. Restaurants, cafés and discos have multiplied rapidly, as have high-rise hotels and apartment blocks, which now spread around the bay to form an almost unbroken ribbon of buildings 10km (6 miles) long.

The stretch of glorious white sand beaches along the **Badia d'Alcúdia** in summer is a mass of bodies soaking

Cattle graze in the wetlands of Parc Natural de S'Albufera

up the sun's rays or sheltering under colourful umbrellas. Although big, crowded and impersonal, the resort, which more or less merges into Can Picafort at the eastern end, does not have the seediness of some of the southern spots. Both remain pretty low-key, if a bit soulless, and are a good option for families with children or teenagers in need of entertainment.

As you drive along the main road, lined with supermarkets, shops and high-rise hotels, signs saying simply 'Platja' lead to the beach. Buses pick up passengers from hotels, and the little Moro Express road train covers some of the distance. The area around **Platja de Moro** is a bit quieter, but it is only just after sprawling **Can Picafort** that development ends, because the sands run out and the shore becomes rocky.

Parc Natural de S'Albufera

About halfway between Port d'Alcúdia and Can Picafort, almost opposite the Hotel Parc Naturel, is the entrance to the **Parc Natural de S'Albufera** (Apr–Sept: daily 9am–6pm; Oct–Mar: 9am–5pm; free). There's a car park a few metres further along. It seems remarkable to find this huge area of wetlands so close to major resorts and it can be a real haven for visitors as well as for birds, more than 200 species of which have been spotted here. A free permit must be picked up from the Reception Centre, about 1 km (½ mile) from the entrance (9am–4pm). The reserve covers 800 hectares (2,000 acres), with walking and cycling tracks through it, and is criss-crossed by a network of canals constructed in the 19th century by a British company that began reclaiming marshland for agriculture, but ran out of money. The area became a protected zone in 1988, one of the first beneficiaries of the new environmental consciousness.

THE CENTRAL PLAIN

The centre of Mallorca is called **Es Pla** (The Plain). Lightly populated, it is little geared towards visitors and doesn't receive many, but it should not be neglected. There are lovely agricultural landscapes with ancient stone farmhouses, olive groves and unassuming old towns. It is known as 'the land of a thousand windmills' and while it's unlikely that anyone has counted, there certainly are a lot of them. They are a characteristic of the island, and many have been restored and put back into use, particularly around Sa Pobla.

Just one of Mallorca's 'thousand windmills'

This route starts at Pollença and visits several inland towns, with a detour to Randa, the 'monastery mountain', but narrow country roads run off in all directions and are worth exploring.

Sa Pobla

The PM220 runs about 12km (8 miles) through fertile farmland to **Sa Pobla**, an unexceptional but pleasant town with several fine old buildings around the main square and a church consecrated to Sant Antoni Abat. A reputable jazz festival takes place in Sa Pobla throughout August.

From here you can continue down the main C713 to **Inca**. It is not a particularly interesting town, but it is worth a visit for its *cellers (see panel on page 72)* and for the factory shop selling Camper shoes.

Binissalem and Sineu

Binissalem is about 8km (5 miles) further down the main road, in the heart of the wine-producing district. You will see vineyards stretching for miles around – particularly attractive in late summer, when grapes are nearly ready for picking. There's a wine festival here at the end of September.

 It's nicer, though, to take the rural (but good) road to **Sineu**, at the centre of the island, the pick of the inland towns. It has an elegant Gothic church, with some lovely reliefs by the Mannerist Gaspar Gener (1563–90), a baroque retable and some interesting modern stained glass. There are also some attractive baronial homes in the town, and a peaceful plaza with good restaurants. On the outskirts of town the **Centre d'Art S'Estació** (Mon–Fri 9.30am–2pm, 4–7pm, Sat 10am–1pm; free) stages interesting exhibitions of contemporary art in a well-converted old station building. In **Costitx**, 7km (4 miles) to the west of Sineu, the **Pla-**

netarium stages astronomical shows (Thur–Sat at 7pm; charge; tel: 971 513 344, 9.30am–1.30pm only) that are both entertaining and educational.

From Petra to the Sanctuaries

From Sineu it's about 11km (6 miles) to **Petra**. One reason  people go to this sleepy little town is to visit the **Casa Museu Fray Juníper Serra** (pre-arranged visits only; tel: 971 561 149). Petra is the birthplace of Fray Serra (1713–84), one of Mallorca's best-known sons, a Franciscan monk who founded numerous missions in California. The museum, run by a dedicated Society of Friends, illustrates these and other New World missions; his house next door is more interesting, a modest place with cell-like rooms and a pretty garden. Wall tiles on the usually closed monastery of Sant Bernardino, opposite, depict the Californian missions; and signs lead to Es Celler *(see page 72)*.

Colourful shutters in Sineu

From Petra it is less than 5km (3 miles) on the MA-3320 to the main Palma road (MA-15). The first town en route in the direction of Palma is Vilafranca de Bonany, known for the production of sweet little tomatoes, garlic, red peppers and melons. A little further along, a turning on the right takes you to **Els Calderers de Sant**

Joan (Apr–Oct: daily 10am–6pm; Nov–Mar: 10am– 5pm; charge), an 18th-century manor house with a chapel, a granary and an extensive estate and farm. You can sample home-made products as part of a tour.

Still heading towards Palma, turn off at Algaida to visit 542-m (1,778-ft) **Puig de Randa**, the highest point on the plain, crowned by the **Santuari de Nostra Senyora de Cura** (accommodation available; tel: 971 660 994). The original sanctuary here was established by the mystic, Ramón Llull (1235–1316). On your way up you pass the Oratori de Gràcia and the hermitage of Sant Honorat. Randa is the centre of a little cluster of sanctuaries. Not far away, the **Ermita de la Pau** has a Romanesque chapel; and just above the village of Porreres you can drive the 4km (2½ miles) up to the **Santuari de Montesió**, which contains a 15th-century marble statue of the Verge de Montesió. There is a bar, restaurant, and accommodation (tel: 971 647 185).

To return to Palma, continue on the MA-15 or get onto the new stretch of motorway (MA-19) at Llucmajor. For the east coast, take the MA-15 towards Manacor, then north to Artà.

Cellers

Anyone interested in the true *cuina Mallorquina* – Mallorcan cooking – should visit a *celler*. These cool basement *bodegas* were originally wine shops and are still lined with huge oak barrels, but have now become restaurants, serving large helpings of island food. They exist all over the island, but there are some especially renowned ones in the inland towns. Inca has about half a dozen, of which Can Amer is the best known. In Sineu, the Ca'n Font on the main square is the place to go, while the best one in Petra is Es Celler (see page 112 for details). They won't suit anyone who wants to eat outside in the sun, but their cavernous depths can be refreshing on a hot day.

Cruising off Cala Mesquida

THE EAST AND SOUTHEAST

The bays and beaches along the east coast have become somewhat overdeveloped and overcrowded, but the resorts are nicer and far less excessive than those around the Bay of Palma, and some spots – harbours such as Port Colom and Cala Figuera – are delightful. There are also two fortified towns in the northeast corner – Artà and Capdepera – and several amazing caves to visit, plus the Bronze Age sites of Ses Païsses (near Artà) and Capocorp Vell, near the south coast.

Artà and Ses Païsses

Artà lies 12 km (8 miles) inland, a fortified town that has retained a friendly, everyday atmosphere, and not become a mere showcase for its historic sites. It has a couple of good hotels with restaurants *(see pages 109 and 140)* and is a good place to stay if you want to escape the razzle-dazzle of the coast.

In a palazzo on the Plaça d'Espanya, the **Museu Regional d'Artà** (Tue–Fri 10am–1.30pm, Sat 11am–1pm; charge) stands next to the town hall and has a number of archaeological finds dating from the Phoenician, Greek and Roman periods, as well as a natural science collection.

The ancient church of the **Transfiguració del Senyor**, with a large rose window above the main portal, is one of Artà's major sites. Beyond, the Via Crucis (Way of the Cross), a broad flight of steps flanked by cypress trees and stone crosses, leads to the **Santuari de Sant Salvador d'Artà**. This great fortress, begun in the 13th century on the remains of a Moorish structure, is enclosed by a battlemented wall, along which you can walk for splendid views across the plain to the coast. You may be lucky and arrive when a recital is being given in the church – a wonderful experience.

27 The prehistoric settlement of **Ses Païsses** (Apr–Oct: Mon–Sat 10am–1pm, 2.30–6.30pm; Nov–Mar: Mon–Fri 9am–1pm, 2–5pm; charge) is about 2 km (1 mile) southeast of Artà on the Camí Corballa. A path leads from the shady car park through an impressive gateway in the Cyclopean wall surrounding the settlement. The ruins, set among holm oaks, include several square foundations, a *talayot* (tower) with a small chamber at its base, and an oval room called a *naveta*, with the remains of several pillars.

Capdepera

Barely 8km (5 miles) east of Artà is the ochre-coloured town of **Capdepera**, its streets filled with flowers. Steps lead from the Plaça d'Espanya to the **Castell de Capdepera** (Apr–Oct: daily 10am–7pm; Nov–Mar: 10am–5pm; charge). The largest castle in Mallorca, it originated in Roman times, the Moors enlarged it and the Christians strengthened it further. Below the defensive wall, from which there is a superb view, stands the 19th-century church of Sant Bartomeu.

From Capdepera a road runs through farmland, past the Canyamel Golf Club, where a new road layout promises urbanisation to come, then winds high above the **Platja Canyamel** development to the **Coves d'Artà** (May–Oct: daily 10am–6pm; Nov–Apr: 10am–5pm; frequent guided tours; charge). Carved out of the sheer cliff face, the caves are less commercialised than the Coves del Drac *(see page 76)* and the limestone rock formations are quite awesome. In summer you can get a boat here from Cala Ratjada.

28 ►

View from Capdepera's castle

Cala Ratjada

It's only 3 km (2 miles) from Capdepera to **Cala Ratjada** (also spelled Rajada), a busy resort built on a grid pattern. It was once the most important fishing harbour on the island, after Palma, but much of the port is now used for leisure and pleasure, as you can see from the boats moored here. There is plenty of accommodation, although much of it is pre-booked by German tour companies; and a rash of fast-food outlets and tourist-tat shops detracts from the atmosphere. However, much of the seafront is attractive, with restaurant tables set among pines and succulents. There is one sandy beach in the centre of town, where good waves attract surfboarders, but most people head through shady pines to the beaches a little further north. The northernmost

Ferry to Menorca

There is a fast passenger ferry from Cala Ratjada to Ciutadella, Menorca, which takes just 75 minutes. There are some good day-return deals available; some include bus transport to Palma. If you are taking a car over, however, you must use the Alcúdia ferry (see page 123 for details).

one is **Cala Mesquida**, with beautiful, protected dunes and excellent surfing waves.

The **Platja de Son Moll** to the south of the resort can be reached via the promenade. Still further south is **Sa Font de Sa Cala**, named after a freshwater spring that flows directly into the sea. Here, a lovely little beach has been completely overwhelmed by two huge hotel complexes.

On a hill above Cala Ratjada's harbour, the **Jardins Casa March** can only be visited by appointment with the tourist office (tel: 971 563 033), but the impressive modern sculpture displayed there makes it worth the effort.

Cala Millor to Porto Cristo

The next resort complex, the largest and loudest on the east coast, is **Cala Millor**, where three separate *calas* merge together along the sandy beach of Son Severa. The resort is still growing, and the neighbouring promontory of **Punta de N'Amer**, a 200-hectare (495-acre) nature reserve, is the only area that hasn't been developed.

The road south passes the Safari-Zoo *(see page 96)* before reaching **Porto Cristo**, an old-fashioned resort with a pleasant, local atmosphere. There is a huge yacht marina, an unremarkable beach and a couple of traditional hotels vying with modern buildings. It's popular with Mallorcan visitors at weekends, and the narrow streets can get clogged.

Most of the tour buses here are ferrying visitors to the **Coves del Drac** (Apr–Oct: daily 10am–5pm; Nov–Mar: 10.45am–3.30pm; charge), south of town. Seven daily tours in summer (five in winter) run through 2km (1 mile) of brightly lit chambers and spectacular formations, culminating with classical music recitals and boat trips on the 177-m (581-ft) long subterranean lake named after Edouard-Alfred Martel, the French speleologist who explored the caves in 1896.

On the road to Manacor, the **Coves dels Hams** (daily 10am–6pm; charge) are competing for subterranean custom, by offering a digital 'virtual adventure'.

Felanitx and the Santuari de Sant Salvador

It's a pleasant drive south through agricultural land, with minor roads leading off to beaches. To the right, just before Porto Colom, is **Felanitx** – you will see watchtowers on the hill as you approach. This was the birthplace, in 1957, of the painter Miquel Barceló, and it is a good place to buy ceramics. There's a lively market on Sunday morning, and an impressive, partly 13th-century church, Sant Miquel.

En route to Felanitx, turn off to the **Santuari de Sant Salvador**, 509m (1,670ft) above sea level. The first sanctuary here was built in 1348; today's structure dates from 1734. On one side of the hill is a 14-m (46-ft) stone cross, and on the other the monument to Cristo Rei (Christ the King). The monastery church contains a fine

Market day in Felanitx

alabaster retable showing scenes from the Last Supper. There are also a number of championship cyclists' jerseys, fading in glass cases along with notes of homage to the virgin. You can drive right up to the sanctuary. There are magnificent views, and accommodation in the Petit Hotel Hostatgería Sant Salvador (tel: 971 515 260), with bright, pleasant rooms and a good restaurant.

Porto Colom to Cala Mondragó

Reached on the PM401 from Felanitx, **Porto Colom** is still a working fishing port, where you can watch the catch brought ashore. There's a strip of beach along the bay but the lack of a significant, sandy beach has ensured that Porto Colom remains a pleasant place, with a pine-shaded promenade and some pretty, pastel-coloured houses. Holiday apartments line the streets inland, but the only real commercial development is around the bay at Cala Marsal, south of the harbour.

Cala d'Or is only 7km (4 miles) further south, but you have to go inland then return to the coast. A resort of many years standing, it has evolved into a huge complex encompassing several different coves and beaches. The architecture is pretty homogeneous – low-rise, flat-roofed and snowy-white. The coves are pretty and the swimming is good, the harbour plays host to some elegant yachts, and there are all the tourist facilities and water sports you could hope for.

If you want to get away from it all, you must go a little further south to **Porto Petro**, an attractive harbour with a yacht club and some nice restaurants; then wend your way to **Cala Mondragó**, which is off the beaten track and practically undeveloped in comparison with most of the coast. It should stay that way, because the two pleasant little sandy beaches are part of the 785-hectare (1,940-acre) **Parc Natural Mondragó** (information office daily 9am–4pm; free;

pre-booked guided tours for groups; tel: 971 181 022), which also encompasses farmland and wetlands. There are walking tracks through the park and lots of opportunities to bird watch and look for wild orchids growing beneath the trees. A couple of inexpensive hotels and beach restaurants are here but it's all very low key.

Santanyí and Cala Figuera

Return to the main road and after 5km (3 miles) you'll come to **Santanyí**, a mellow little town of honey-coloured sandstone with one gate, Sa Porta Murada, remaining from the fortified walls. The elongated Plaça Major, where there are some friendly cafés, is dominated by the huge church of **Sant Andreu Apostel**, which has a famous, ornate organ, and the adjoining **Església de Roser**, the original 14th-century parish church (both daily 6–7.30pm only; free). There's an

Cala Mondragó

Fishing boats moored
at Cala Figuera

arty feel to Santanyí, with several exhibition venues, and a number of antiques and ceramics shops.

Cala Figuera is delightful, **33** a fishing port with neat green-and-white houses and a walk-way alongside the boathouses right at the water's edge. A handful of leisure boats bob in the waters, but they do not outnumber or outshine the working vessels. There are plenty of restaurants and some accommodation but the tourist industry has not got out of hand.

Journey's End

Back to the main road again, and the first stop after Santanyí **34** is **Botanicactus** (Jun–Aug: daily 9am–7pm; Sept–Oct and Feb–May: 9am–5.30pm; Nov–Jan: 10.30–4.30pm; charge). It is said to be one of the best botanical gardens in Europe, and contains 1,500 different plant species. It's not all cacti – there's an artificial lake surrounded by palms, and a stunning assortment of indigenous flowers.

Some 7km (4 miles) away is **Colònia de Sant Jordi**, one of Mallorca's earliest resorts. Its pleasant harbour is the starting point for trips to Cabrera *(see panel opposite)*, and you can walk around the dunes to the south of the bay. To the west of Sant Jordi the sandy stretch of **Platja Es Trenc** is now a pro-tected area, so major development will not be permitted.

The main road west from Santanyí, through a flat, agri-cultural landscape where many of the windmills have been

renovated with brightly coloured sails, goes to **Campos**, a ◀⑤
friendly town with two huge, sandstone churches. The
Església Parroquial Sant Julià contains a painting by Mur-
illo (1617–82) but it is usually only open for the 8pm mass.

The road then heads to **Llucmajor,** an ancient town with
a few striking *Moderniste* buildings. If you want to go straight
to Palma, the new stretch of motorway will take you almost
the whole way. Otherwise, follow signs to **Capocorb Vell** ◀⑥
(Fri–Wed 10am–4.30pm; charge), the best-known Bronze Age
site in Mallorca. The foundations of 28 enormous buildings
can be seen, and at the edge of the settlement are two massive
talayots and three round towers.

You can drop down to **Cabo Blanc**, where a lighthouse ◀⑦
stands on a rocky promontory. From here the road runs
along a fairly dull stretch of coast towards the **Platja de
Palma**. **S'Arenal**, the largest resort, merges into **Les Mer-
avelles** on a 7-km (4-mile) strip of packed beaches, fast-food
outlets, high-rise hotels, high-throttle discos, English pubs,
Murphy's bars and German beer halls. Approaching the
yacht harbour of **Ca'n Pastilla**, the road becomes pedestri-
anised and more pleasant – and then you are back in Palma.

Cabrera

Cabrera, an uninhabited island 17km (10 miles) south of Cap de Ses
Salines, has been a nature reserve since 1991 (boat trips Apr–Oct: daily;
must be reserved in advance, tel: 971 649 034). It's just 7km (4 miles)
by 5km (3 miles) in extent with a rocky coast and rugged limestone centre where a track leads 72m (236ft) up to the castle. There are two little bays, good for swimming and snorkelling. Bring your own supplies, or
opt for lunch on the boat, because there is nowhere to buy food or
water. During the Napoleonic Wars, Cabrera was used to house French
prisoners, and it later quartered Spanish soldiers.

WHAT TO DO

SPORTS

Most outdoor activities in Mallorca revolve around the water and there is a great range of things to do, including sailing, windsurfing, kitesurfing, paragliding, water-skiing, snorkelling, fishing and, of course, swimming. However, walking, climbing and bird watching are catching up in popularity, drawing thousands of visitors to the island, especially in spring and autumn, when the mild weather makes walking a pleasure, and numerous species of migrating birds delight birdwatchers. Mallorca is also a great place for cycling, horse riding and golf.

Sailing

The Balearics are a sailing paradise. Among those who recognise this are King Juan Carlos, who sails the royal yacht around the coast every summer, and movie star Michael Douglas. The island has a wealth of safe harbours and some 40 marinas, and thousands of foreign visitors keep their own boats here all year round.

You can **hire** various kinds of craft for an hour, day or week at many beaches and hotels (but you must produce proof of qualification for a self-drive motor boat). The **Asociación Provincial de Empresarios de Actividades Marítimas de Baleares** is the biggest yacht charter company (tel: 971 727 986, www.apeam.com). The **Centro Náutico Port de Sóller**, Platja d'En Repic, Port de Sóller, tel: 609 354 132, www.nauticsoller.com, is recommended for all kinds of water-based activities. The **Escuela Nacional de Vela**

Bathers at Cala de Sa Calobra

Calanova, Avinguda Joan Miró 327, Palma, tel: 971 402 512, offers intensive beginners' courses; as does **Centro Náutico Port de Sóller** *(see previous page)*. **Sail and Surf Pollença**, Passeig Saralegui, Port de Pollença, tel: 971 865 346, www.sailsurf.de is a prestigious club that offers instruction for beginners and more advanced sailors.

Windsurfing and Water-Skiing

There are windsurfing schools, with equipment hire, at several of the larger resorts. **Centro Náutico Port de Sóller** and **Sail and Surf Pollença** *(see above)* both offer windsurf hire and tuition, as does **Llaüts**, Camino San Carlos 6A, Port d'Andratx, tel: 971 672 094, www.llauts.com. On the east coast, windsurfing facilities are available at Cala Millor and Cala d'Or. Water-skiing equipment can be hired on many beaches, including Cala Millor, Can Picafort and Port d'Alcúdia. **Ski Club Calanova**, Carrer Condor 22, Son Ferrer, Santa Ponça, tel: 971 100 328, is recommended.

Scuba Diving

Mallorca's crystal-clear waters, especially in the shallow coves on the south and east coasts, are ideal for diving. Scuba-diving equipment is available for hire, if you have a qualification from your home country. The **Federación Balear de Actividades Subacuaticas**, Puerto Deportivo Cala Nova, Palma, tel: 971 708 785, www. fbdas.com, can give information and advice. The numerous scuba diving clubs include three in the southwestern corner: **Dragonera Dives (Aqua Marine Diving)**, Port d'Andratx, tel: 971 674 376, www.aqua-mallorca-diving.com; **Scuba Activa**, Sant Elm, tel: 971 239 102, www.scuba-activa.com; and **Big Blue Diving**, Palmanova, tel: 971 681 686, www.bigbluediving.net, with numerous sites for people of all ability levels. In Alcúdia there's Oceanos, tel: 971 549 957, www.5oceanos.com; and in the northeast,

Windsurfers have a wonderful time in Mallorca

Mero Diving, Cala Ratjada, tel: 971 565 467, www.mero-diving.com, is well established.

Boat Trips

There are trips available from various points along the west coast. In Port de Sóller, **Barcos Azules**, Passeig Es Través 3, tel: 971 630 170, www.barcosazules.com runs a variety of trips around the rugged coast and tiny bays, including Sa Calobra. Boat trips operate from most ports, some using glass-bottomed boats. The tourist office produces a leaflet listing dozens of them, with contact details, but you will also see them advertised, and be given flyers, in the harbours.

Walking and Climbing

The Mallorcan landscape is perfect for dedicated hikers and more leisurely walkers. April and May, with a wild profusion of flowers, are the best months and September and

October are good, too. In the hotter months, start early in the day or make use of the long evenings. Needless to say, correct footwear is essential and common sense will tell you that a supply of water, a wide-brimmed hat and sunscreen are wise precautions.

The **Serra de Tramontana** makes for the most dramatic scenery, especially on the climb to Castell d'Alaró *(see page 56)* and between the Monasteri de Lluc and the coast. In the southeast corner, there are numerous walking trails through the pine groves, marshlands and dunes of the **Parc Natural de Mondragó** (information office open daily 9am–4pm, tel: 971 181 022). These are on

Looking along the coast from Cap Formentor

flatter terrain and more gentle than those in the northwest. The tourist office in Sóller, tel: 971 638 008, produces a leaflet outlining 20 walking excursions in the northwest of the island. There are walkers' maps available in La Casa de la Mapa, Carrer Sant Domingo 13, Palma and the bookshop of the Fundació La Caixa, Plaça Weyler 3, Palma, which also stocks a helpful book called *48 Walks in Mallora* by Rolf Goetz (Rother Walking Guides) and other excellent books on walking in Mallorca. In addition, there is a website, www.mallorca-camins.info, that has lots of information.

There are also serious rocks in Mallorca, for serious climbers. Contact the **Federació Balear de Muntanyisme**, www.fedme.es; **Grup Excursionista de Mallorca**, www.gemweb.org (both websites in Catalan and Spanish only); or **Secció Muntanya Club Pollença**, Plaça Major 1, Pollença, tel: 971 532 108.

Climbing is popular in Mallorca

Golf

There are twelve 18-hole golf courses on Mallorca, and all are challenging enough for even the best players. You can also hire equipment and take lessons. The beautifully landscaped **Son Vida Golf**, tel: 971 791 210, hosts the Balearics' Open, while the course at **Golf Santa Ponça**, tel: 971 690 211, is one of Europe's longest. On the east side of the island, **Canyamel**, tel: 971 564 457, and **Capdepera**, tel: 971 565 875, are both popular. For further information, contact the **Federació Balear de Golf**, Avinguda del Rei Jaume III 17, Palma, tel: 971 722 753.

Bird Watching

Mallorca is one of the most rewarding bird watching sites in Europe. The island's resident birds are enticing enough, but it's the visiting species that generate most excitement. Migrant birds stop off in spring – as many as 200 species have been spotted – and some stay for the summer. The most rewarding sites are the **Tramuntana** region, where rare black vultures and other birds of prey can be seen; the **Parc Natural de Mondragó** (tel: 971 181 022) for marine birds; and the

Parc Natural de S'Albufera (tel: 971 892 250, http://mallorcaweb.net/salbufera), probably the best wetland site on any Mediterranean island, for the widest variety of all.

Horse Riding
There are a number of small ranches and stables scattered all over the island, and some *agroturisme* properties offer treks or can arrange them for you. A few of the reputable riding schools are: **Escuela de Equitación de Mallorca**, Carretera Sóller Km 12.2, tel: 971 613 157; **Rancho La Romana**, Peguera, tel: 971 687 084; and **Centro de Hípica Formentor**, Hotel Barceló, Platja de Formentor, tel: 971 899 100.

Cycling
Bikes can be hired at most resorts. Check brakes and tyres and make sure a lock and puncture kit are included. There are lots of rustic little bike route signs dotted around the island and some main roads have clearly delineated cycle tracks. In Palma, bikes can be hired by the hour or day at Av. Gabriel Roca 15, tel: 610 355 570, www.palmaonbike.com (they also organise bike tours, and hire rollerblades and kayaks). In Puerto de Pollença, try BPP, Carrer Temple Fielding 3, tel: 971 866 857.

Spectator Sports
Football is as popular in Mallorca as in other parts of Spain and there are dozens of clubs. The premier league team, **Real Mallorca**, plays at Son Moix stadium at Camí del Rei, Palma (www.rcdmallorca.es). Tickets usually available on the day.

   Bullfights *(corridas)* exist, but they are not the big deal they are in some parts of Spain. They're staged on summer Sunday afternoons in Palma's Plaça de Toros.

   Horse races are held every Sunday, all year round, at the **Hipòdrom de Son Pardo** near Palma. Betting is organised through a centralised tote system.

SHOPPING

Shopping in Mallorca is more expensive than it used to be, but you will still find some bargains, particularly if you are looking for leather goods or glass. For designer labels, however, **Carrer Verí**, in Palma's old town, has some smart boutiques, as well as several antique shops; and **Carrer Estanc**, off the **Passeig de Born**, has a number of chic clothing and interior design shops. **Avinguda Jaume III** is the capital's major shopping street, lined with leather and clothing shops as well as a huge branch of Spain's biggest department store, **El Corte Inglés**, which has a supermarket in the basement.

Lovely Leather

The Balearic Islands are justly famous for their leather industries. Excellent shoes, belts and bags and some of the finest

Some items on sale in Pollença

Books

An extraordinary treasure trove of English books can be found at **Fine Books,** Carrer Morey 7, Palma, tel: 971 723 797, three floors of jumbled volumes, everything from first editions to nearly new paperbacks, prints and old photos.

leather and suede jackets come from the islands. The focus of the leather industry is Inca, where you can shop at the factory outlets or the local market, which is fun, although the goods may not be any cheaper than you will find in Palma.

If you like shoes, then you'll love shopping in Mallorca. You can go to the factory shop of the quirky shoe company **Camper** (on the main road around Inca), whose highly individual shoes have become well known. Camper also has outlets in Palma, in Avinguda Jaume III and Carrer Sant Miquel. Less trendy, but extremely attractive and comfortable are *abarcas*, the slipper-like sandals made in Menorca that have been worn by peasants for centuries.

Linen
Mallorca's embroidered table and bed linens are quite attractive, and the market in Llucmajor is a great place to find them. Other towns known for good-quality embroidery are Manacor, Pollença and Artà. In Palma, you will see a number of shops selling fine, hand-embroidered linen – and a lot of others selling machine-made versions.

Glassware, Pottery and Pearls
High-quality **glassware** has been made on the island for centuries. The **Gordiola Museu del Vidre** factory and museum, outside Algaida on the Palma–Manacor road, is a good place to go. You can watch glass blowing and see some of the antique pieces on which many current products are based. They have a showroom in Palma, at Carrer Victoria 2.

Pottery is another traditional craft. There are two main types of cooking pots: *ollas* (round) and *greixeras* (flat and shallow). **Siurells** are small, clay figurines painted in red and green, based on Phoenician and Carthaginian originals.

Mallorcan cultured (artificial) **pearls**, Perlas Majorica, manufactured in Manacor, are exported in huge numbers. The best place to buy them is at the (well-signposted) **Pearl Centre** on the main road just outside the town, where you get a tour of the factory and have the biggest choice. You can buy them all over the island, however, including in Palma, at Avinguda Jaume III 11, and prices do not vary much from shop to shop. But don't imagine they are cheap because they are artificial.

Food and Drink

Olive selection

Mallorca is known for its herbal **liqueurs**, and the popular aperitif, **Palo Tunel**, made in Bunyola, is a novelty. Look for the bright green bottles with the train logo, and decide if you want the sweet variety *(dulce)* or the dry *(amargo)*. Also worth trying is the orange liqueur, **Angel d'Or**, made in Sóller; as is wine from Binissalem, as you are unlikely to find it outside the island. **Olive oil** from around Bunyola is an excellent buy, not cheap but fine quality. **Olives**, too, are worth taking home. For a selection of Mallorcan varieties, in all shapes, sizes and shades, acquire a plastic container and fill it up by selecting from the large tubs on market stalls. For specialised foodstuffs the most fascinating place is in the old-fashioned little **Colmado Santo Domingo** in Carrer Sant Domingo, near the city tourist office. You'll spot it immediately as it's festooned with hams, sausages and strings of peppers and garlic.

Markets

Weekly markets are held all over the island, where everything from fresh farm produce (including live chickens) to leather bags, household linen, pots and pans, sunglasses and sandals are for sale. They usually start fairly early in the morning and finish around 1pm. Particularly lively ones are held in Alcúdia on Tuesday and Sunday, in Pollença on Sunday and Sóller on Saturday. On Saturday morning in Palma the Baratillo, flea market, is fun, even if you don't want to buy.

ENTERTAINMENT AND NIGHTLIFE

A monthly guide to events in Palma can be obtained from tourist offices. Otherwise there are listings in the *Mallorca Daily Bulletin* and a free listings publication, *V&mos365*, which you can also read online (www.vamos-mallorca.com).

Palma has a lively classical music scene. There are two excellent concert halls, the Sala Magna and the Sala Mozart, in **L'Auditorio**, Passeig Marítim 18, tel: 902 332 211 for bookings, www.auditoriumpalma.es. The Ciutat de Palma Symphony Orchestra has its home here and there's a varied programme of orchestral music, ballet, jazz and opera. The **Teatre Principal**, Carrer del la Riera 2, tel: 971 713 346, www.teatreprincipal.com, stages opera, classical concerts and jazz; and the **Teatre Municipal**, Passeig de Mallorca 9, tel: 971 739 148, hosts dance as well as contemporary drama and films. Concerts are also held in the **Centro Cultural de la**

Misericòrdia in Via Roma, tel: 971 713 346, and, in summer, in the music room of the **Palau March**, tel: 971 711 122, www.fundbmarch.es. Free outdoor concerts – jazz, rock and classical – are held in the beautiful setting of the **Parc de la Mar** below the city walls on some summer evenings. A bar serves drinks and snacks and there's a party atmosphere.

Late Night Line-up

The bars, clubs and discos in the big resorts thump with loud music all night long and would be hard to miss. Needless to say, they rise and fall in favour, and predicting next season's hottest spot would be unwise. They are mostly geared to the teen and early-twenties age groups and there is no shortage of leaflets and posters trying to tempt customers.

Otherwise, most of Mallorca's nightlife is to be found in Palma, where the best clubs are **Abraxas** (formerly **Pacha)**,

The Abaco bar is a novelty that's well worth a visit

which has a split-level terrace and top DJs; and **Tito's**, popular with those who want to dance till dawn. Both are on the Passeig Marítim. Remember that the action doesn't really start until around midnight.

Outside the clubs, much of Palma's nightlife takes place in late-night bars, many of them in the Sa Llotja area, where most of the restaurants are. The kitsch **Abaco**, Carrer Sant Joan (off Apuntadors), tel: 971 714 939, with its exotic decor, caged birds, operatic background music and expensive cocktails, is an experience. The **Atlántico**, Carrer San Feliu 12, is also popular for cocktails, but with rock instead of opera. **Jazz Voyeur Club**, Carrer Apuntadors 5, is a small, intimate place that offers a mixture of live jazz and blues from 10pm, except Monday; **Blues Ville**, Carrer des Moros 3 (just off Carrer l'Estanc), plays, as you would expect, blues. **El Garito**, Dàrsena de Can Barbarà (near the Club de Mar), tel: 971 736 912, has a retro feel and good jazz. The **Yuppi Pub**, at Avinguda Joan Miró 106, is a popular gay music bar.

Music Festivals

Summer is the time for music festivals, most held in beautiful historic buildings. The best known one is the Deià International Music Festival. Most performances are in the stunning setting of Son Marroig (tel: 971 639 178, www.dimf.com/concerts). The Chopin Festival is held in the cloister of La Cartuja in Valldemossa (tel: 971 612 351, www.festivalchopin.com>; and the Festival de Pollença (tel: 971 534 012 or 971 535 077; www.festival pollenca.org) attracts international musicians to the lovely cloister of Sant Domingo. There is a summer music festival with performances in Palma's Castell de Bellver (tel: 971 728 841) and in the Jardins Fundació March in Cala Ratjada (tel: 971 563 033). Sa Pobla hosts an international jazz festival in August (tel: 971 544 111, www.ajsapobla.net/jazz) and Palma stages events in L'Auditorio on various dates as part of the Jazz Voyeur Festival.

CHILDREN

Sandy beaches and calm, safe waters ensure that children can be happy on the beach for days at a time. But if that begins to pall, there are plenty of alternatives. The big resorts have a lot to offer in terms of entertainment such as water parks; they are quite expensive, but you can easily spend a whole day in them, which means you get your money's worth.

Splashing around at Cala Ratjada

In S'Arenal, **Aqualand**, Palma–Arenal motorway, exit 13, tel: 971 440 000, www. aqualand.es, with its mega-water slides, claims to be the biggest aquatic park in Europe. Its associate **Aqualand Magaluf**, Carretera Cala Figuera, tel: 971 130 811, is another huge park, with a Boomerang slide. **Western Park**, Carretera Cala Figuera–Sa Porrassa, Magaluf, tel: 971 131 203, www.westernpark.com, has high-diving exhibitions, falcon displays and a cowboy show as added attractions. All open daily at 10am and there are special buses from the nearby resorts. In the north, **Hidropark**, Avinguda Tucán, Port d'Alcúdia, tel: 971 891 801, caters for younger children as well.

Marineland Mallorca, Costa d'en Blanes, Calviá, Palma–Andratx motorway, exit 10, tel: 971 675 125, www.marine land.es, has dolphins, sea lions, flamingos, toucans and performing parrots as well as a reptile house. Performing dolphins are a controversial subject.

For older children and teenagers, there is **Magaluf Karting**, Ctra Cala Figuera-Sa Porrassa, tel: 971 131 134, next to the

Aquapark; and **Can Picafort Karting**, near Alcúdia, tel: 971 850 748, www.kartingcanpicafort.com. Children of all ages love trips in the **Nemo Submarine**, which leaves from Magaluf, tel: 971 130 244 (free transport from all over the island).

Safari-Zoo, Ctra Porto Cristo–Cala Millor, tel: 971 810 909, www.safari-zoo.com, on the east coast is usually a hit. The monkeys, antelopes, elephants, giraffes and rhinos can be observed from a mini-train, or from your own car. Fascinating for adults and children is the huge **Palma Aquarium**, Platja de Palma, motorway exit 10, tel: 971 746 104, www. palmaaquarium.com (buses 15, 23 and 25 from Palma stop right outside). The **Acuarium de Mallorca**, Carrer Vella, Porto Cristo (next to the Coves del Drac), tel: 971 820 971, is smaller but also appeals to older children. The animals and the birds of prey at **La Reserva Puig de Galatzó** *(see page 46)* are popular; and **Jumaica Tropical Park**, Carretera Porto Colom–Porto Cristo, tel: 971 833 979, is another winner. The vast model dinosaurs in the **El Valle de los Dinosaurios**, Ctra Palma–Manacor Km 16 usually win approval.

Most children – apart from the very young – enjoy exploring caves. There are the **Coves del Drac** at Porto Cristo *(see page 76)*, the

Light effects at the Coves d'Artà

Coves d'Artà at Canyamel *(see page 75)*, and the **Coves dels Hams**, Ctra Porto Cristo–Manacor, which stage a digital 'virtual adventure'.

Museums aren't high on most kids' wish lists, but many of them enjoy the **Museo de Muñecas Antiguas** (Dolls' Museum) in Carrer Palau Real, behind Palma's cathedral.

Calendar of Events

5–6 January: Three Kings (Reyes Magos) Procession in Palma.

16–17 January: Sant Antoni Abat festival in Palma, Artà, Sa Pobla and Manacor; a procession of animals to be blessed by their patron saint.

19–20 January: Sant Sebastià celebrated in Palma and Pollença, where the *cavallets* (small papier-mâché horses that the dancers strap round their hips) perform in a procession.

February: Carnival (Carnaval) celebrated in many towns and villages, with fancy dress parades and general revelry. This is a pre-Lent festival so dates vary depending on Easter.

March–April: Semana Santa (Holy Week) is celebrated in Palma and throughout the islands with solemn processions. In Pollença the Devallament (Lowering) sees a figure of Christ brought down from the Oratori on the hill.

8–10 May: Cristians i Morus festival, also called Ses Valentes Dones, in Sóller re-enacts a battle in 1561 when local women fought against invading Turkish pirates.

13 June: Sant Antoni de Padua festival in Artà. Lively festivities involve *cavallets (see above)* and black demons that cavort around the streets.

15–16 July: Día del Verge del Carmen, the patron saint of fishermen and sailors, is celebrated in many ports with processions on the water. Palma, Port de Sóller and Cala Ratjada are the principal venues.

last Sunday: Sant Jaume in Alcúdia is a big religious and secular festival.

24 August: Sant Bartomeu is celebrated in Capdepera and Montuïri with horse races and devil dancers.

28 August: Sant Agustí fiesta in Felanitx, with *cavallets* and *cabezudos* (big heads).

September – first Sunday: Processó de la Beatá in Santa Margalida.

last Sunday in September or first in October: the Festa des Butifarró in Sant Joan, with folk dancing and feasting on the famous Mallorcan black pudding *(butifarró)*.

31 December: Festa de Standa in Palma commemorating the Christian reconquest of the island under Jaume I in 1229, with a procession.

EATING OUT

Restaurants in Mallorca cover a wide spectrum, from the excellent to the mediocre, from the local to the international. You will find traditional, rural cooking – the hearty *cuina mallorquina* – as well as ubiquitous Spanish dishes like *paella* and *gazpacho* that are very popular although they have little to do with the island. There has also been a recent emphasis on Basque cooking, which is regarded as one of the best regional cuisines in Spain; and there are refined dishes with a French flair in the more expensive restaurants. Several top-notch chefs are working on the island and, while a meal in one of their restaurants is not cheap, it is considerably less expensive than it would be in one of the European capitals. At the other end of the market there are, of course, such staples as chicken and chips, pizza, bratwurst and sauerkraut for people who like to stick with what they know. The list of recommended restaurants on page 107 will help you make some informed choices.

Cuina Mallorquina

Much of the best cooking derives from simple, country fare, cooked in olive oil and made from whatever fresh ingredients are in season. *Cuina mallorquina* reaches its height in *cellers (see page 72)* but can be found in many other places, too. A meal usually starts with a dish of multi-coloured, oddly-shaped and quite delicious olives and a basket of rough-textured bread being brought to the table. There is sometimes a small charge for this, sometimes it is on the house.

Sopas mallorquinas – invariably referred to in this plural form – is a combination of vegetables, olives, garlic and sometimes pork. It is more like stew than soup, and makes a substantial first course. The *sopas* are usually served in an

Trying local dishes at lunchtime in Palma's restaurant district

earthenware bowl, or *greixera de terra*, which in turn gives its name to a complete range of casseroles: *greixonera de peix*, is a fish stew, and *greixonera d'alberginies* (or *berenjenas* in Castilian) is a wonderful aubergine concoction.

Another speciality is *tumbet*, a dish of peppers, aubergines, tomatoes and potatoes, coated in beaten egg and baked in the oven. This usually features as a first course, but can be very filling so should be followed by something fairly light. *Frit mallorquí* is a tasty mixture of strips of fried liver and kidney, peppers and leeks.

Meat

Every rural family on the island once kept pigs, and many still do. Pork and its by-products are a mainstay, therefore, including *botifarra* (a spicy sausage, either white or dark), *sobrasada*, a bright red, pork-and-red-pepper-sausage with a consistency rather like pâté, and *jamón serrano* or *jamón*

Caldereta de langosta

iberico, a delicious cured ham, cut from a whole piece hanging from the ceiling.

Other popular dishes are *llomb amb col* (pork with cabbage and raisins); and *arròs brut* (rice with pork or chicken). *Lechona asada* (roast suckling pig) is really a Christmas dish but may sometimes be found on menus at other times.

You don't see a great many cows in Mallorca, so there's not a lot of beef in the restaurants, although some of the more expensive places serve delicious steaks. Chicken – *pollo* – is fairly common, though, and goat – *cabrito* – turns up on country menus, usually grilled, sometimes in a stew. Rabbit *(conejo),* is popular, sometimes served in a *greixonera* (stew), or *à la plancha* – grilled, and accompanied by *allioli,* a garlic mayonnaise; *conejo con caracoles*, rabbit with snails, is a favourite dish.

Snails *(caracoles)* are something of an acquired taste, but one that the islanders acquired long ago. At times they can be a free source of protein: after it has rained you'll see people out carrying string bags full of sand. They're looking for snails, which they clean by leaving them for several days in the sand, before cooking them and then eating them with *allioli.* Purists insist that true *allioli*, which is sometimes also served with the bread and olives that arrive at the start of a meal, should be made simply with oil and garlic, without the addition of eggs.

Fish

Really fresh fish and seafood are becoming something of a luxury on Mallorca. The seas have been over-fished and local fishermen, in any case, could not keep up with demand in summer. If you ask, waiters will usually tell you honestly that much of the fish they serve is imported, frozen, from Spain's Atlantic ports. *Salmonete* (red mullet) is caught locally, so are sardines *(sardinas)* and some of the *langostas*, spiny lobsters that are found on many menus. Locally caught *cap roig* – scorpion fish – is the choice Mallorcan fish; the cheeks are considered a great delicacy. *Caldereta de langosta* (*llagosta* in Mallorquí), a delicious lobster casserole, is a Menorquin dish, and an expensive one, that appears on some Mallorcan menus. *Zarzuela de mariscos* can be excellent – a thick stew of shellfish, tomatoes, garlic, wine and almonds.

Farmed trout *(trucha)*, sole *(lenguado)* and hake *(merluza)*, which are imported into the islands frozen, also feature. Squid *(calamares)*, cuttlefish *(sepia)* and octopus *(pulpo)* cooked in a variety of ways, are also widely available. *Calamares en su tinta* is squid cooked in its own ink; *a la romana* means it is cut into rings and fried in batter – excellent when

Bread and Oil

Mallorca, whose landscape is dotted with ancient, gnarled olive trees and once-functional windmills, is renowned for its bread and oil – so much so that Tomás Graves, the son of Robert, has written a whole book about it. The bread is dense and biscuit coloured, the oil thick and rich and green. So it is not surprising that *pa amb oli*, bread and oil (pronounced *pamboli*), is served everywhere. It is simply toasted bread rubbed with garlic, sprinkled with salt and lubricated with olive oil. As a refinement it is also rubbed with fresh tomatoes *(pa amb tomàquet)* and served with cheese, local ham, *sobrasada (see page 99)* or even tuna. Cafés called *pambolierias* will give you your chosen ingredients on a large platter, plus a bottle of oil, and leave you to make yourself a tasty, filling and economical snack.

fresh and not over-battered. *Bacalao* is cod, salted and dried, and not to everyone's taste, but when well prepared it can be good, especially in *esqueixada*, a salad of tomatoes, onions, beans and shredded salt cod.

Fruit for dessert

There is also fruit, of course; sweet melons, juicy oranges, peaches and nectarines, fresh figs and grapes, all the better because they are locally grown and have ripened in the field, not in transit.

Sweets and Puddings

Home-made *crema catalana*, or its mass-produced cousin, known as *flan*, is as ubiquitous in the Balearics as the mainland, but there are also some wonderful sweet pastries and the almond and honey desserts that are a legacy of the Moorish occupation. Fig cake, a rich, dark brown confection with the consistency of Christmas pudding, is particularly popular in and around Sóller, a town also known for its *picos de marzapan* – little white pyramids of marzipan. Vegetarians should be aware that lard *(saim)* is an essential Mallorcan ingredient. It is a key element in the *ensaimada*, the light, airy pastry that's rolled up like a turban, dusted with sugar, and eaten for breakfast, sometimes dipped in coffee.

Drinks

Wine is usually drunk with meals, much of it imported from the Spanish mainland; Riojas and varieties from the Catalan Penedès region feature prominently. But island wines are good, too, and some restaurants (especially the *cellers*) specialise in them. Most come from the region around Binissalem, which lies between Palma and Inca. Spanish beer is also popular. Fresh orange juice *(zumo de naranja)* is refreshing and delicious; and those who like the flavour of almonds should try *horchata de chufa*, a milky drink made from ground almonds that is served ice cold in summer. A local aperitif is *palo*, made from carobs and herbs and produced in Bunyola; and Angel d'Or, made in Sóller, is a local orange liqueur.

Eating Habits

Local people eat late; lunch is between 1.30 and 4pm, and any time before 9.30 or 10pm is regarded as a bit early for dinner. However, restaurateurs, aware that northern European visitors like to eat earlier, have adapted their timetables accordingly. Remember that a restaurant that may look empty and unloved at 8pm may be packed and popular by 10pm. As breakfast is insubstantial – coffee and toast or a croissant – lunch is often the main meal. Islanders generally have three courses, but it's perfectly acceptable to share a first course, or to order *un sólo plato* – just a main course.

Many restaurants offer a *menú del día*, a daily set menu that is a real bargain; this is always available at lunchtime, and occasionally in the evening as well. For a fixed price (around €12), you get three courses – a starter, often soup or salad, a main dish and dessert, which is usually ice-cream, a piece of fruit or a *flan*, plus bread and a glass of wine, beer or bottled water. In restaurants where local

Binissalem produces a good range of wines

Alfresco dining

people are eating, you will notice that many of them order the *menú*, an indication that it is not one specially designed for tourists.

Reservations are necessary only at the more expensive restaurants or places that are popular for Sunday lunch. Prices may or may not include 7 percent IVA. They sometimes include service – look for *servicio incluido* on the bill. If not, it is customary to leave a 10 percent tip.

Tapas

Tapas, the snacks that have become popular far beyond the borders of Spain, form a major part of eating out in Mallorca – at least in the bigger towns. They are still eaten as snacks, with drinks, which was their original role, but it is now common for a selection of these small dishes, or *raciones*, which are larger portions, to take the place of a main meal and this can be a relatively inexpensive way to eat. The advantage is that it allows you to be adventurous without making too many mistakes. The size of portions varies quite a lot, so be guided by a waiter as to how many dishes to order. As well as meatballs *(albóndigas)* and mushrooms *(champiñones)* you can try stuffed squid *(calamares rellenos)*, *pimientos de padrón* – small, green peppers grilled whole and sprinkled with sea salt; spicy *chorizo* or *espinacas à la catalana* – spinach cooked with garlic, anchovies, raisins and pine nuts. All are served with fresh bread to mop up the sauces and complement the strong flavours.

Bars and Cafés

Bars and cafés are an important institution in Spanish life. In towns, some open at first light to cater for early-morning workers and most are open by 8.30am for breakfast. One of the great pleasures of the Mediterranean is sitting in a square in the morning with a *café con leche* (coffee with milk) or *café solo* (black coffee) and a croissant or *ensaimada* and watching a town come to life. In resorts, however, where many bars are open late at night and many tourists breakfast in their hotels, you may have more difficulty finding somewhere for an early coffee.

Wines and spirits are served at all hours. It is usually 10 percent cheaper to have a drink at the bar rather than at a table. Sitting on a stool at the bar can make you feel like one of the locals, too, although it is not as relaxing as taking your place at an outside table and watching the world go by.

Can Joan de S'Aigo in Palma, Miró's favourite café

TO HELP YOU ORDER

Could we have a table?	¿Nos puede dar una mesa, por favor?
Do you have a set menu?	¿Tiene un menú del día?
I would like...	Quisiera...
The bill, please	La cuenta, por favor

DECIPHERING THE MENU

agua	water	poco hecho	rare
vino	wine	al punto	medium
leche	milk	buen hecho	well done
cerveza	beer	asado	roast
pan	bread	a la plancha	grilled
entremeses	hors-d'oeuvre	al ajillo	in garlic
ensalada	salad	picante	spicy
tortilla	omelette	salsa	sauce
pescado	fish	cocido	stew
mariscos	shellfish	jamón serrano	cured ham
langosta	lobster	chorizo	spicy sausage
calamares	squid	morcilla	black pudding
mejillones	mussels	bocadillo	sandwich
anchoas	anchovies	arroz	rice
atún	tuna	verduras	vegetables
bacalao	dried cod	champiñones	mushrooms
cangrejo	crab	judías	beans
pulpitos	baby octopus	espinacas	spinach
trucha	trout	cebollas	onions
carne	meat	lentejas	lentils
cerdo/lomo	pork	queso	cheese
ternera	veal	postre	dessert
cordero	lamb	helado	ice cream
buey/res	beef	azúcar	sugar
pollo	chicken	flan	caramel custard
conejo	rabbit		

PLACES TO EAT

The following basic price guide (which is only approximate) is for a three-course à la carte meal for one, with a glass of house wine:

€€€€ over 70 euros   €€ 30–50 euros
€€€ 50–70 euros   € below 30 euros

PALMA

Caballito del Mar €€ *Passeig de Sagrera 5, tel: 971 721 074.* The place to go for fish and shellfish cooked to suit your requirements. There's an outside terrace just around the corner from lively Plaça Sa Llotja, but it's separated from the waterfront by the busy main road.

Ca'n Carlos €€€ *Carrer de S'Aigua 5, tel: 971 713 869.* On a quiet pedestrian street, off Jaume III, this atmospheric place specialises in *cuina mallorquina*. Dishes include roast lamb and aubergine stuffed with shellfish. Closed Sun and second week of August.

Celler Sa Premsa € *Plaça Bisbe Berenguer de Palou 8, tel: 971 723 529.* This is a real institution, that has been operating for 60 years. A great ambience, good, filling, everyday food with a wide selection of Mallorcan classic dishes. Closed Sat and Sun.

El Pesquero € *Moll de la Llotja s/n, Port de Palma, tel: 971 715 220.* A variety of fish and seafood dishes served on a broad deck overlooking the port. Cheerful atmosphere. Many people come here just for an early evening drink and a portion of tapas.

Es Rebost d'es Baluard €€–€€€ *Plaça Santa Catalina 9, tel: 971 719 609.* Stylishly presented modern Mallorcan cuisine, including innovative dishes such as sticky rice and rabbit. Next to Es Baluard Museu d'Art Modern i Contemporani. Closed Sun.

Forn de Sant Joan €€ *Carrer Sant Joan 4, tel: 971 728 422.* Dining rooms on three floors in the heart of the old town restaurant area. À la carte Mediterranean dishes available, but basically it's upmarket tapas – and very nice too. Also does a good gourmet menu for €15 from 1–4pm. Closed Mon.

Koldo Royo €€€ *Avinguda Ingeniero Gabriel Roca 3 (Passeig Marítim), tel: 971 732 435.* Considered by many to be Palma's best restaurant, this elegant place overlooking the waterfront serves delicious and highly imaginative basque cuisine. Bookings essential. Closed Sun.

La Bóveda €–€€ *Carrer Botería 3, tel: 971 714 863.* There's usually a queue of tourists outside at 8pm each evening, waiting for the door to open, but this big, lively place is equally popular with locals, who come later. There's a wide selection of excellent tapas and main courses. Another branch, with more modern decor, is found at *Passeig Sagrera 3, tel: 971 720 026.* Both closed Sun.

Porto Pí €€€–€€€€ *Avinguda Joan Miró, 174 y Garita, 25, tel: 971 400 087.* Hidden away, just back from the port below Bellver Castle, this old Mallorcan house has a Michelin star. International dishes are prepared using fresh local ingredients and plenty of creative flair. Very stylish. Closed Sat lunchtime and Sun.

Taberna Lizarran € *Carrer Enric Alzamora 2, tel: 971 727 443; Carrer Brondo s/n, tel: 971 721 819.* Sister bar/restaurants, both busy, cheerful and noisy, serving great tapas in huge portions. Locals outnumber tourists. Don't expect a smoke-free zone, though.

13% € *Carrer Sant Feliu 13a, tel: 971 425 187.* Just of Passeig des Born, this attractive wine bar serves excellent salads and plates of ham and cheese as well as fish and meat courses and a good variety of wine by glass or bottle. Closed Sun.

THE WESTERN CORNER

Andratx

La Dorada €€ *Avinguda Mateo Bosch 31, Port d'Andratx, tel: 971 671 648.* Right on the seafront with an attractive upstairs dining room and outside table. Specialises in fish but doesn't neglect meat dishes. and there's almond cake with almond ice cream for pudding.

Banyalbufar

Son Tomás €€ *Carrer Baronia 17, tel: 971 618 149*. A small bar-restaurant whose terrace commands outstanding views of the coast. Fish comes directly from the boats in the cove; paella and the *arroz negro* (black rice) are recommended. Closed Tue and Nov–Feb.

THE WEST COAST

Deià

Ca'n Quet €€–€€€ *Carretera Valledemossa–Deià, tel: 971 639 196*. This renowned restaurant, linked to hotel Es Molí *(see page 135)*, specialises in international cuisine with a local flavour. People flock here from Palma for dishes such as giant prawns in puff pastry, especially at Sunday lunchtime. Closed Mon and Nov–Apr.

El Barrigon Xelini € *Archiduc Lluis Salvador 19, tel: 971 639 139*. Loud and lively, this popular place on the main road specialises in tapas and they come in all varieties. The stuffed squid is extremely good; the staff are friendly and casual; there's an outside terrace open in the summer months.

El Olivo €€€–€€€€ *Son Canals, tel: 971 639 011*. One of the top restaurants on the island, attached to La Residencia Hotel *(see page 136)*. Delicious nouvelle cuisine and excellent wine cellar. Try the gastronomic menu if you feel flush. Dining on the terrace is a delight. Open daily for dinner only.

Es Racó d'es Teix €€€ *Carrer Sa Vinya Veia 6, tel: 971 639 501*. Chef Josef Saueschell produces nouvelle cuisine in satisfying portions and has won a Michelin star. The *ballontine conejo* (medallions of rabbit) is delicious. The food and the fairytale gardens with ravishing views make it easy to forgive the fact that it's a tad pretentious.

Jaume €€€ *Archiduc Lluis Salvador 24, tel: 971 639 029.* This friendly, family-owned place on the main road prepares generous helpings of Mallorcan food. Go for seafood or classics like *tumbet.* Book if you want to eat on the terrace. Dinner only; closed Mon.

Sóller

QD €€ *Carrer Sant Ramón 1, Port de Sóller, tel: 971 633 934.* Lots of interesting salads and fish dishes, and a delicious tart made with the local Angel d'Or liqueur. Outside tables only, right by the harbour.

Sa Cova €€ *Plaça Constitució 7, Sóller, tel: 971 633 222.* Pleasant restaurant on the main square. Serves good *conejo* (rabbit), which appears on many menus in the area, and seafood stew – *cazuela.*

Ses Porxeres €€–€€€ *Carretera Palma–Soller, Km17, Bunyola, tel: 971 613 762.* Beautiful place near the Jardins d'Àlfabia. Specialities include game, fish stew and lamb cutlets grilled on hot rocks. Booking essential. Closed Sun evening, Mon, and August.

THE NORTH

Alcúdia

Es Canyar €€ *Carrer Major 2, tel: 971 547 282.* Good food served all day, starting with breakfast. There's a delightful hidden courtyard and the vaulted interior is hung with original paintings.

Cala Sant Vicenç

Cavall Bernat €€€ *Carrer Maressers 2, tel: 971 530 250.* An excellent restaurant in the Cala Sant Vicenç hotel *(see page 138).* Refined Mediterranean cooking and a fine wine list. There's a set menu of delicious tastes. Open daily for dinner; closed Dec–Jan.

Pollença

Clivia €€ *Avinguda Pollentia 7, Pollença, tel: 971 533 635/971 534 616.* An elegant lace-curtained setting close to the main square, in which to enjoy Mallorcan cuisine – fish soup, baked *lubina* (sea bass) and mountain ham are favourites. Closed Wed.

Font del Gall €€ *Montesion 4, Plaça Almoina, tel: 971 530 396*. Owned by a Scottish family, the Font del Gall, behind Plaça Major, serves a good range of dishes in a friendly atmosphere, indoors or out on a terrace. Dinner Sun–Fri and Sun lunch; Sat dinner Jul–Sept.

Il Giardino €€ *Plaça Major 11, Pollença, tel: 971 534 302*. Great Italian food served in a pleasant dining room and outside on the square, where you must book to get a table. Sunday lunch here is a social occasion.

Latitud N €€ *Carrer Costa I Llobera 11, Pollença, tel: 971 531 294*. Run by a young couple from Argentina, this restaurant offers delicious international food in a wonderful indoor contemporary space with creatively lit lounge bar areas, at the same price as local Spanish restaurants (mains around €15). Closed Mon.

Port de Pollença
Stay €€–€€€ *Moll Nou s/n, tel: 971 864 013*. A smart restaurant right in the centre of the port that has been operating for years. Fish is the first choice but there are imaginative meat dishes too, including lamb and pigeon ravioli. Open every day of the year.

Tribeca €€ *Carretera Formentor 43, tel: 676 763 994*. Prides itself on a varied menu using fresh local ingredients. Wild mushrooms, stuffed aubergines and local trout may feature. Vegetarian dishes always available. Open all year for dinner.

THE EAST AND SOUTHEAST

Artà
Ca'n Epifanio €€–€€€ *Carrer Castellet 7, tel: 971 829 555*. In the Sant Salvador hotel this restaurant has a small menu that includes such *nouveau* goodies as *mille feuille* of lobster. Closed Tue.

Cala d'Or

Port Petit €€€ *Avinguda Cala Longa, tel: 971 643 039.* This place has great views of the harbour and an adventurous menu that, according to owner-chef Gérard Deymier, changes according to 'the season, the market and the imagination of the chef'. Closed Tue.

Cala Figuera

Es Port € *Carrer Virgen del Carmen 88, tel: 971 165 140.* Eat inside or out, overlooking the bay. Spanish and Mallorcan specialities, fresh fish and good pizzas. One in a row of inviting-looking establishments. Closed Tue.

Cala Ratjada

Ses Rotjes €€€–€€€€ *Carrer Rafael Blanes 21, tel: 971 563 108.* This restaurant, in the hotel of the same name, has a Michelin star and is delightful. Although fresh fish is their speciality, they don't neglect the meat dishes. The extensive wine list is not over-priced. You can eat in a sheltered courtyard in summer. Reservations advisable. Closed mid-Nov–mid-Mar except Christmas/New Year.

THE CENTRAL PLAIN

Inca

Celler Ca'n Amer €€ *Carrer Pau 39, tel: 971 501 261.* The best known of Inca's famous *cellers*, this family-run establishment has a long tradition of serving large portions of robust island food and a vast selection of wines.

Petra

Es Celler €€ *Carrer de l'Hospital 46, tel: 971 561 056.* Huge and cavernous restaurant serving heaped plates of traditional food, including meat roasted in a traditional wood oven.

Sineu

Celler de Ca'n Font €€ *Sa Plaça, Sineu, tel: 971 520 313.* Another one of the traditional *cellers*, Ca'n Font, in a hotel of the same name *(see page 141)*, specialises in *sopas mallorquinas*, roast suckling pig and rice dishes.

A–Z TRAVEL TIPS

A Summary of Practical Information

A

ACCOMMODATION (See also *CAMPING*, and the list of *RECOMMENDED HOTELS* on pages 133–141)

Hotel prices are not government-controlled, but rates are posted at reception desks and in rooms. Off-season, you can often get lower rates, although many hotels in resort areas close between November and March. In season, the majority of large resort hotels are block-booked by package tour operators. Breakfast is often but not always included in a room rate; check before booking. A value-added tax (IVA) of 7 percent is added to the total.

Accommodation ranges across a broad spectrum, although there are few *pensions* (guest houses). *Hostales* (modest hotels) are graded from one to three stars while *hoteles* (hotels) are rated from one to five stars. Grades are more a reflection of facilities than quality: some two-star places can be superior to others with four. A new category – the *hotel d'interior* – has been introduced. These are small hotels (no more than eight rooms) which must be in traditional buildings, however minimalist their interior decoration may be.

Small hotels in rural settings and refurbished farmhouses and manor houses are called *finca* or *agroturisme* properties. They range from rustic to luxurious and many have minimum 4- or 7-day stays; contact Agroturisme Balear, Avinguda Gabriel Alomar i Villalonga 8a, 2º, Palma, tel: 971 721 508, www.agroturismo-balear.com, for details. All-in package deals are the cheapest option and, while accommodation is usually in the busiest resorts, it can provide an economical base for exploring the island. If you want to rent a villa or apartment there are numerous agencies: www.majorcanvillas.com is a reliable one. Finally, there is the option of staying in a monastery or sanctuary, of which there are about 15 (the *Where to Go* section gives details of several) and the tourist office in Palma *(see page 130)* can provide a full list. These are fairly austere but extremely economical and popular with local people and outdoor enthusiasts.

I would like a single/ double room	**Quisiera una habitación sencilla/doble**
With/without bathroom and toilet/shower	**con/sin baño/ducha**
What's the rate per night?	**¿Cuál es el precio por noche?**
Is breakfast included?	**¿Está incluído el desayuno?**

AIRPORT *(Aeropuerto)*

Palma de Mallorca's massive **Son Sant Joan Airport** (PMI) is about 9km (5½ miles) east of the city centre (tel: 971 789 000, 24-hr information line: 902 404 704; www.aena.es). Taxis and buses link the airport with Palma. Bus No. 1 leaves the airport every 15–20 minutes from 6.10am to 1.10am (2.15am in summer), running to Plaça d'Espanya, and to the port with stops en route (fare currently €2). There is a bus stop outside the car park, in front of the Arrivals Hall. Taxi is a lot faster than the bus, taking around 15–20 minutes. They line up outside Arrivals; the approximate fare is €18.

B

BICYCLE AND SCOOTER HIRE *(Bicicletas de aquiler)*

A practical and enjoyable way to see the island is to hire a bicycle, and this can be done in most resorts – hotels and tourist offices have leaflets, and you'll be handed flyers in the street. Mopeds and scooters are also available, but you'll need a special licence. Prices vary widely, so shop around. Remember that a helmet is compulsory when riding a motorcycle, whatever the engine size. Ask for a helmet and for a pump and puncture kit, in case you get stuck with a flat tyre many kilometres from your hotel. In Palma, go to Avinguda Gabriel Roca 15, tel: 610 355 570, www.palmaonbike.com. Pro Cycle Hire will deliver your bike direct to your resort hotel if arranged in advance; tel: 971 866 857 or check www.procyclehire.com.

BUDGETING FOR YOUR TRIP

Mallorca has become more expensive in recent years, particularly for those hit by the current poor sterling/euro exchange rate. All prices below are approximate and given only as a guide.

Getting there. Air fares vary enormously. Flights from the UK with a budget airline can vary from around £70 return off-season to £190 or more in high season. Scheduled flights can be as low as £130 if you book well in advance, but anything up to £300 if you make a relatively late booking. The cheapest flights are usually available via the Internet, or by taking a chance on a last-minute offer.

Accommodation. Hotels can be more expensive than on the Spanish mainland *(see approximate prices in Recommended Hotels, page 133)*. Rates for two sharing a double room during high season can range from as low as €55 in a *hostal* to as much as €400 at a top-of-the-range hotel. A comfortable, pleasant 3-star hotel will cost about €100–€120. Rates drop considerably out of season.

Meals. The *menú del día*, a fixed price midday meal, is usually an excellent bargain, costing around €12 for a reasonably good three-course meal with one drink included. In a bar a continental breakfast (fresh orange juice, coffee and croissant) will cost around €5; a coffee €1.50–€2. The average price of a three-course à la carte meal, including house wine, will be about €35 per person. You can pay considerably less, but at top restaurants you may pay more than twice that much. The price of wine has increased: you will pay about €2.50–€3 for a glass of wine in a smartish bar.

Attractions. Most museums and galleries charge an entry fee of around €3–5. Entry to La Real Cartuja, Valldemossa costs €8; the Coves del Drach around €10. Water parks are more expensive, around €18–20 (children €12). A 2-hour trip in a glass-bottomed boat costs around €15 (children half-price).

Ferries. Inter-island ferries between Mallorca and Menorca are reasonable for foot passengers (about €75 return), but quite expensive if you take a car, about €250 for a vehicle and two passengers.

C

CAMPING

Pitching a tent on beaches and parkland is illegal and you will be asked to move on. You may be able to camp on private land, but be sure to ask permission from the owner first.

There are two official camp sites, both in the north of the island. Club San Pedro, Colonia Sant Pere, tel: 971 589 031, open mid-May to mid-September, is 1.5km (1 mile) from the beach, with a swimming pool, showers, bar/restaurant, and supermarket. Sun Club Picafort, Platja de Muro, tel: 971 537 863, is open all year. It is within walking distance of the beach and facilities include swimming pools, tennis courts, showers and baths, bars/restaurant, supermarket and disco. Both sites have a capacity for 500 pitches, but Sun Club Picafort is by far the better of the two in terms of site, facilities and maintenance. Camping is also permitted at the Santuario de Lluc, tel: 971 871 525.

CAR HIRE (Coches de alquiler)

The bus service is good, but if you want to travel a good deal around the island, hiring a car is advisable. Major international companies – Avis, Hertz, Budget, Europcar – and Spanish national companies have offices at the airport and in Palma as well as in the major resorts. Many have weekly specials which can work out as little as €30–35 per day. Rates are seasonal, and usually lower if organised in advance over the Internet. Third-party insurance is included, but comprehensive insurance – *todo riesgo*, is usually extra. Be aware that insurance may not cover you for off-road driving. In addition

I'd like to rent a car. for one day/week. Please include full insurance.	**Quisiera alquilar un coche. por un día/una semana. Haga el favor de incluir el seguro a todo riesgo.**

to value-added tax (IVA) of 15 percent, an extra tax of €5 a day, controversially introduced to raise local revenue, is also payable.

Hirers must be at least 21 and have held a licence for six months. Hire companies will accept your national driver's licence.

Avis: Passeig Marítim 16, Palma, tel: 971 286 233, www.avis.es.

Betacar: Passeig Marítim 19, tel: 971 737 589, www.betacar.biz.

Barceló: Av. Cala Marçal 16, Porto Colom, tel: 971 824 858, www.servicios-barcelo.com.

Hertz: Passeig Marítim 13, Palma, tel: 971 734 737, www.hertz.es.

Hiper: C. Elcano s/n, tel: 971 866 768, www.hiperrentacar.com.

CLIMATE (Clima)

The sea is pleasantly warm for swimming from June to October. July and August can be scorching and humidity may be high. Spring and autumn bring walkers and bird watchers and those who enjoy sight-seeing in cooler temperatures. Mallorca enjoys a mild winter, and many hotels stay open during the winter months. It can be chilly and wet at times but a wall of mountains along the northwest coast protects the rest of the island from the worst of the winter weather.

The average temperatures below apply to Palma, but do not vary greatly throughout the islands, except in the mountainous areas.

	J	F	M	A	M	J	J	A	S	O	N	D
°C	10	11	12	14	17	22	24	24	22	18	14	12
°F	50	51	54	58	63	71	76	76	72	65	57	53

CLOTHING (Ropa)

In summer you only need lightweight cotton clothes – although in June and September you may need a jacket or sweater for the evening. Remember also to take a sunhat and something with sleeves to cover your shoulders. During the rest of the year a light jacket and an umbrella will come in handy.

Although the tendency is towards casual dress, some restaurants, bars and clubs object to men wearing shorts and T-shirts and women being too skimpily dressed. Don't offend local sensibilities by wearing unsuitable clothes in city streets, museums or churches.

Walking shoes or good-quality trainers are advisable, of course, if you are planning any long treks.

CRIME AND SAFETY (See also EMERGENCIES)

Spain's crime rate has caught up with that of other European countries and the Balearics have not been immune, although they remain one of the safest places in Europe. Be on your guard against purse-snatchers and pickpockets near Palma Cathedral and around the Plaça Major at night, and in markets and other crowded places. Take the same precautions as you would at home. In Palma, report thefts and break-ins to the Policía Nacional, elsewhere to the Guardia Civil. You need a police report for insurance purposes.

I want to report a theft.	**Quiero denunciar un robo.**

D

DRIVING (En coche)

Road conditions. There is a stretch of motorway around the city and the bay, west towards Andratx, ending at Peguera, and east to Llucmajor. Another motorway goes north via Inca to the Sa Pobla Pollença interchange, with plans to extend it to Alcúdia. There is also a tunnel through the mountains (toll charged) from Sóller towards Palma. There's a good straight road running east–west across the island. Secondary roads are narrow but generally good; on the mountainous northwest coast there are numerous hairpin bends.

Rules and regulations. Drive on the right, overtake on the left, yield to vehicles coming from the right. Seat belts are compulsory. Children under 10 must travel in the rear. Speed limits are 120 km/h (75 mph) on motorways, 100 km/h (60 mph) on two-lane highways, 90 km/h (56mph) on other main roads, 50 km/h (32 mph), or as marked, in densely populated areas.

Traffic police. Roads are patrolled (strictly) by the Guardia Civil de Tráfico, on motorcycles. Fines are payable on the spot. The permitted blood-alcohol level is low and penalties are stiff.

Fuel. Service stations are plentiful. Petrol *(gasolina)* comes in 90 (super lead-free) and 98 (lead-free super plus) grades. Diesel fuel is widely available. Petrol is slightly cheaper than in the UK.

Parking. Underground car parks have made parking easier in Palma (the one in Av. Antoni Maura by the Cathedral as you enter town is a good one), and it is less of a problem elsewhere. Most towns have metered areas, denoted by a 'P' and blue lines on the road.

Mechanical problems. Garages are efficient, but repairs may take time in busy areas. For emergencies, call the Real Club Automóvil (tel: 902 404 545) or tel: 062 for Guardia Civil traffic police.

Road signs. Most are standard pictographs, but you may also see the following; the subsequent phrases may also be useful.

Aparcamiento	Parking
Desviación	Detour
Obras	Road works
Peatones	Pedestrians
Peligro	Danger
Salida de camiones	Truck exit
Senso único	One way

Useful expressions:

¿Se puede aparcar aquí?	Can I park here?
Llénelo, por favor.	Fill the tank please.
Ha habido un accidente.	There has been an accident.

E

ELECTRICITY *(Corriente eléctrica)*

The 220-v system is now standard. Sockets (outlets) take round, two-pin plugs, so you will probably need an international adapter plug (available at airports).

EMBASSIES AND CONSULATES *(Embajadas y consulados)*

The following are consulates:

UK: Carrer Convent dels Caputxins 4, Palma, tel: 971 712 445.

US: Edificio Reina Constanza, Porto Pi 8, Palma, tel: 971 403 707.

Ireland: Carrer Sant Miquel 68, Palma, tel: 971 719 244/722 504.

Australia, Canada, New Zealand and South Africa have no consuls in Mallorca; their embassies in Madrid are:

Australia: Plaza Descubridor, Diego de Ordás 3, Madrid tel: 913 536 600.

Canada: Edificio Goya, Calle Núñez de Balboa 35, Madrid, tel: 914 233 250.

New Zealand: Plaza de la Lealtad 2, Madrid, tel: 915 230 226.

South Africa: Calle Claudio Coello 91, Madrid, te: 914 363 780.

Where is the British/American   **¿Dónde está el consulado**
consulate?   **británico/americano?**

EMERGENCIES *(See also EMBASSIES, HEALTH and POLICE)*

General emergency number (police, fire, ambulance): 112

National Police: 091

Municipal Police: 092

Guardia Civil (traffic): 062

Ambulance: 061

Fire: 080

Those who respond are usually able to understand English.

Police!	**Policía!**
Help!	**Socorro!**
Fire!	**Fuego!**
Stop!	**Deténgase!**
Go away!	**Váyase!**

G

GAY AND LESBIAN TRAVELLERS *(Viajeros gay)*

The Balearics are among the most hospitable places in Spain for gay travellers. Mallorca has a number of establishments, including hotels, bars, discos and restaurants, that cater for gays or are gay-friendly. For information on the best places to go, contact Ben Amics, Carrer Conquistador 2, Palma, tel: 971 715 670, www.benamics.com.

GETTING THERE

Air Travel *(see also Airports)*. Palma de Mallorca's airport is linked by regular scheduled non-stop flights from London, Dublin, Berlin and Frankfurt, with frequent flights from many other European cities; from Belfast you need to go via Gatwick/Heathrow and/or Barcelona or Madrid. Flights from the US and Canada also go via London airports and Barcelona or Madrid; flight time from New York is approximately 10–12 hours. In the US contact Iberia, tel: 1-800 772 4642, www.iberia.com; Continental Airlines, tel: 1-800 231 0856, www.continental.com. In Canada, contact British Airways, tel: 1-800 AIRWAYS, www.ba.com; Iberia, tel: 1-800 423 7421 (website as above). From Australia and New Zealand, flights usually go via London, where you can get a connecting flight to Palma.

For information on scheduled flights from the UK, contact Iberia, tel: 0870 609 0500, www. iberia.com; British Airways, tel: 0844 493 0787, www.ba.com; Spanair, tel: 902 131 415, www. spanair.es. From Eire, Aer Lingus, tel: 0818 365 000, www.aerlingus.com. Numerous budget airlines, including easyJet www.easyJet.com, fly to Palma from airports all over the UK. Excellent bargains may be available if you travel at very short notice, both for flight-only tickets and for packages that include accommodation. Booking via the Internet is usually the cheapest method for flight-only tickets.

By Sea. Car ferries operate daily from Barcelona and Valencia to Palma. The slower, overnight trip takes about 8 hours on Acciona-Trasmediterránea (Moll de Paraires, Estació Marítim 2, tel: 902 454 645 or 971 702 300/971 366 050 in Palma; www.trasmediterranea.es); during peak holiday season it also operates a faster ferry, which takes 4 hours. Baleària has services from Barcelona to Palma (4½ hours) and to Alcúdia, which takes 5½ hours (tel: 902 160 180/966 428 700, www.balearia.com). Faster yet is the Buquebus (Moll de Paraires, Estació Marítim 3, tel: 902 414 242 in Barcelona or 971 400 969 in Palma; www.arrakis.es), which takes 3½ hours.

H

HEALTH AND MEDICAL CARE *(Salud; atención médica)*

Standards of hygiene are generally high; the most common problems visitors encounter will be due to an excess of sun or alcohol. Bottled water is always safest, and is available, cheaply, almost everywhere. *Agua con gas* is carbonated, *agua sin gas* is still.

First-aid personnel *(practicantes)* make daily rounds of the larger resort hotels; some hotels have a nurse on duty. Many resorts have medical centres *(centros medicos)*, privately-run institutions which must be paid on the spot, in cash or by credit card (roughly €50/£45 a consultation).

It is always advisable to take out insurance to cover the risk of illness or accident when on holiday. Residents of EU member states are entitled to reciprocal health arrangements on production of the European health insurance card (www.ehic.org) available free online in your home country), but it does not cover all eventualities.

Pharmacies *(farmácias)* are open during normal shopping hours, but there is at least one – the *farmácia de guardia* – open all night in Palma and in the large resorts. In small towns, it may be difficult to find an after-hours pharmacy. A list of the pharmacy on rota duty is posted in chemists' windows. Spanish pharmacists are highly trained and generally speak at least some English; they can dispense drugs over the counter that would often need a prescription elsewhere.

In Palma, the Farmácia March at Avinguda Joan Miró 186, tel: 971 402 133/971 605 008 is open 24 hours a day, 365 days a year.

Emergency medical assistance can be obtained by dialling **112** or **061** (Ambulance), or tel: 971 295 000 – Creu Roja (Red Cross). There is also a 24-hour medical helpline, tel: 900 221 022.

Major hospitals in Palma include: Hospital Universitario Son Dureta, Carrer Andrea Doria 55; tel: 971 175 000. Hospital de la Creu Roja Espanyola, Carrer Pons i Gallarça 90, tel: 971 751 445.

Where's the nearest (all-night) chemist?	**¿Dónde está la farmácia (de guardia) más cercana?**
I need a doctor/ dentist.	**Necesito un médico/ dentista.**
sunburn/ sunstroke	**quemadura del sol/ una insolación**
an upset stomach	**molestias de estómago**

L

LANGUAGE *(Idioma; lenguaje)*

While Castilian Spanish is the national language of Spain, a local form of Catalan – Mallorquí – is widely spoken, and almost all islanders speak both. Most street signs appear only in Catalan. If you know some Spanish, you'll be fine. English and German are widely understood in resort areas.

| Do you speak English? | ¿Habla usted inglés? |
| I don't speak Spanish. | No hablo español. |

M

MAPS *(Mapa = country/regional map; plano = town map)*

The maps of the island and cities available at all tourist information offices should be sufficient, even for those travelling by car. Even though some roads are not labelled by number or name on the map, they are easy to identify. A good place for more specific maps is La Casa de la Mapa, Carrer Sant Domingo 13, Palma.

| Do you have a map of | ¿Tiene un plano de la |
| the city/island? | ciudad/isla? |

MEDIA *(Periódico = newspaper; revista = magazine)*

In the main tourist areas most English and German newspapers are sold on the day of publication. The Paris-based *International Herald Tribune* and the European edition of the *Wall Street Journal* are available on the day of publication. *USA Today* is widely available, as are the principal European and American magazines.

The *Majorca Daily Bulletin*, an English-language publication geared mainly to a British ex-pat readership, has a What's On section. There's also a free listings magazine, *V&mos365*. For Spanish speakers, the *Diario de Mallorca* is useful.

Most hotels and bars have television, usually tuned to sports, and broadcasting in Castilian, Catalan (from Barcelona) and Mallorquí. Satellite dishes are sprouting and most tourist hotels offer multiple channels (German, French, Sky, BBC, CNN, etc). Reception of the BBC World Service radio is usually good. The Palma local radio station broadcasts in English 24 hours a day on 103.2 FM.

MONEY *(Dinero)*

Currency. Since 2002, Spain's monetary unit has been the euro (€), which is divided into 100 cents. Bank notes are available in denominations of 5, 10, 20, 50, 100, 200 and 500 euros, and there are coins for 1 and 2 euros and for 1, 2, 5, 10, 20 and 50 cents.

Currency exchange. Banks are the best place to exchange currency as they offer the best rates and charge no commission. A large number of travel agencies exchange foreign currency, and *casas de cambio* stay open outside banking hours. Both banks and exchange offices pay slightly less for cash than for travellers' cheques. Always take your passport as proof of identity.

ATMs. Perhaps the easiest way of obtaining cash but check how much your bank will charge you for doing so.

Travellers' cheques. The majority of hotels, shops, restaurants, and travel agencies cash travellers' cheques, and so do banks, where you're likely to get a better rate (you will need your passport).

Where's the nearest bank/ currency exchange office?	¿Dónde está el banco más cercano/la oficina de cambio más cercana?
I want to change some dollars/pounds.	Quiero cambiar dólares/ libres esterlina.
Do you accept travellers' cheques?	¿Acepta usted cheques de viajero?
Can I pay with this credit card?	¿Puedo pagar con esta tarjeta de crédito?

O

OPENING HOURS *(Horario)*

Most shops and offices are open from 9am to 1pm and again from 5pm until 8pm. Many museums and other tourist attractions maintain the same schedule, although increasingly the more popular ones are staying open all day. Large supermarkets and department stores usually stay open all day and some until 10pm. Banks generally open Mon–Fri 9am–2pm, and Sat 9am–1pm in winter only.

Restaurants serve lunch from 1–3.30pm. In the evenings timing depends on the kind of customers they expect. Local people usually eat between 9.30 and 11pm. Places catering for foreigners may function from 7pm, and many serve food throughout the afternoon.

P

POLICE *(Policía)*

Dial 092 for municipal police and 091 for national police. The general emergency number is 112. The municipal police station in Palma is located at Carrer Ruíz de Alda 8.

POST OFFICES *(Correos)*

Identified by yellow and white signs with a crown, post offices are for mail; you can't phone from them (www.correos.es). The postal system is pretty reliable and efficient. Special delivery is always a good idea if you want to make really sure of a speedy delivery. Opening hours are usually Monday to Friday 9am–2pm. The grand main post office in Palma in Carrer Constitució 5 (off Passeig des Born), tel: 902 197 197, opens Mon–Fri 10am–10pm, Sat 11am–10pm, Sun noon– 10pm. Stamps *(sellos)* are also sold by tobacconists *(estanco/tabacos)* and by most shops selling postcards. Post boxes are unmissable – large and yellow, with 'Correos' written down the side.

Where is the (nearest) post office?	**¿Dónde está la oficina de correos (más cercana)?**
A stamp for this letter/ postcard, please.	**Por favor, un sello para esta carta/tarjeta.**

PUBLIC HOLIDAYS *(Fiestas)*

The following are official public holidays. There are a number of other holidays, usually saints' days, dotted throughout the year.

1 January	Año Nuevo	New Year's Day
6 January	Epifanía	Epiphany
20 January	San Sebastián	St Sebastian's Day
1 May	Día del Trabajo	Labour Day
25 July	Santiago Apóstol	St James's Day
15 August	Asunción	Assumption
12 October	Día de la Hispanidad	National Day
1 November	Todos los Santos	All Saints' Day
6 December	Día de la Española	Constitution Day
8 December	Inmaculada Concepción	Immaculate Conception
25 December	Navidad	Christmas Day

Movable dates:

Late March/April	Jueves Santo	Maundy Thursday
Late March/April	Viernes Santo	Good Friday
Late March/April	Lunes de Pascua	Easter Monday
Mid-June	Corpus Christi	Corpus Christi

T

TELEPHONES *(Teléfonos)*

Spain's country code is 34. The local area code is 971 and must be dialled before all phone numbers, even for local calls.

The telephone office is identified by a blue and white sign. You can make direct-dial local and international calls from public telephone booths in the street. Many only operate with a phone card *(tarjeta telefónica)*, which can be purchased at any *estanco* (tobacconist's). International telephone credit cards can also be used. Instructions for use are given in several languages in the booths. You can also make calls at public telephone offices called *locutorios*. An attendant will place the call for you, and you pay afterwards.

To make an international call, dial 00 for an international line plus the country code plus the phone number, omitting any initial zero. Calls are cheaper after 10pm on weekdays, after 2pm on Saturday, and all day Sunday.

TIME DIFFERENCES *(Huso horario)*

The Balearics keep the same time as mainland Spain, which is one hour ahead of GMT, so Spanish time is generally one hour ahead of London, the same as Paris and six hours ahead of New York.

TIPPING *(Propinas)*

A service charge is sometimes included on restaurant bills *(servicio incluido)*. If not, it is usual to tip waiters 10 percent, and taxi drivers a similar amount; leave a few coins, rounding up the bill, in a bar. Give porters, chambermaids and hairdressers about €2.

TOILETS *(Servicios)*

There are many expressions for toilets in Spanish: *baños, servicios, lavabos, aseos, wc* and *bater*. The first three are the most common. Toilet doors usually have a 'C' for *Caballeros* (gentlemen), an 'S' for *Señoras* (ladies). Public toilets exist in some large towns but they are rare; most bars will allow you to use their facilities.

TOURIST INFORMATION OFFICES
(Oficinas de información turística)

Tourist Offices Abroad
Canada: 2 Bloor Street West, Suite 3402, Toronto, Ontario M4W 3E2, tel: 1416-961 3131, www.tourspaintoronto.on.ca.
UK: 22–23 Manchester Square, London W1M 5AP, tel: 020 7486 8077; brochure line, tel: 0891 669 920, email: info.londres@ tourspain.es; www.tourspain.co.uk.
US:Water Tower Place, Suite 915 East, 845 North Michigan Avenue, Chicago, IL 60611, tel: 312-944 0216/642 1992; 8383 Wilshire

Boulevard, Suite 960, Beverly Hills, CA 90211, tel: 213-658 7188; 666 5th Avenue, 35th floor, New York, NY 10103, tel: 212-265 8822; 1221 Brickell Avenue, Miami, FL 33131, tel: 305-358 1992; www.spain.info/us/tourspain.

Tourist Offices in Mallorca

The general information number in Palma is tel: 902 102 365.

Palma: Airport, tel: 971 789 556; for information on the whole island: Plaça de la Reina 2, tel: 971 712 216.

Municipal Tourist Offices (for information on Palma only): Casal Solleric, Passeig des Born 27, tel: 902 102 365; Plaça d'Espanya (Parc de les Estacions), tel: 902 102 365.

Cala Ratjada: Plaça dels Pins, tel: 971 563 033.

Sóller: Plaça d'Espanya s/n, tel: 971 638 008.

Pollença: Carrer Santo Domingo 17, tel: 971 535 077.

TRANSPORT *(Transporte público)*

Mallorca has a reliable and comprehensive transport system serving almost all towns and villages. You can get a bus and train timetable from the tourist information offices in Palma and Sóller *(see above)*, or tel: 971 177 771 or from a helpful information office in the Estació Intermodal (to the right of the entrance).

Bus *(autobús)*. Mallorca is well served by bus lines; its vehicles are clean, efficient and easy to use and drivers are generally helpful. Destinations are marked on the front of the bus and each town has its own bus station or terminal. In Palma, services begin their journeys in the Estació Intermodal, the new combined bus and railway station across the road from Plaça d'Espanya. Long-distance buses are run by Transportes de les Illes Baleares (http//tib.caib.ed) and Palma services by Empresa Municipal de Transports (www.emtpalma.es). There is a set fare for city journeys (€1.25) and you buy your ticket on the bus. There is also the hop-on hop-off Turistbus.

Train *(tren)*. Mallorca has two narrow-gauge lines. The first starts from the Estació Intermodal and goes to Inca and Manacor, with some trains running to Sa Pobla; while the more picturesque one runs from a suitably old-fashioned station next door, and links Palma and Sóller. It makes seven runs in each direction every day. For Inca trains, tel: 971 177 777; for Sóller trains, tel: 902 364 711/971 754 631.

Metro. Palma has a new metro system but as it runs across the north of the city, from Plaça d'Espanya to the University, it is not very useful for tourists. See www.urbanrail.net for a metro map.

Ferries. Passenger ferries to Menorca go between Cala Ratjada and Ciutadella (Cape Balear Cruceros, tel: 971 818 517/971 818 668). The journey takes about 75 minutes; some deals offer inclusive bus journeys to and from Palma. Car ferries run twice a day (except Sat) between Port d'Alcúdia and Ciutadella and take around 2¾ hours (Iscomar Ferries; tel: 902 119 128/971 437 500; www.iscomar.com). Baleària has daily connections between Alcúdia and Ciutadella and Maó, tel: 902 160 180, www.balearia.com.

Taxi. Taxi rates are metered and displayed in several languages on the window. In Palma: Radio Taxi: tel: 971 755 440; Taxi Palma Radio: tel: 971 401 414. In Sóller: tel: 971 638 484; In Pollença: tel: 971 866 213. In Cala Ratjada: tel: 971 819 090.

> How much is it to the centre of town?   **¿Cuanto es al centro?**

TRAVELLERS WITH DISABILITIES *(Los discapacitados)*

Palma airport and most modern hotels have wheelchair access and facilities for travellers with disabilities. For more general information, consult the online magazine *Able*, Craven Publishing 15–39 Durham Street, Kinning Park, Glasgow GW1 1BS, tel: 0141 419 0044, www.ablemagazine.co.uk.

VISAS AND ENTRY REQUIREMENTS (See also EMBASSIES AND CONSULATES)

Citizens of the UK, US, Canada, Australia and New Zealand need only a valid passport to enter Spain and the Balearics for a stay of up to 90 days. Citizens of South Africa need a visa. Full information on passport and visa regulations is available from the Spanish Embassy in your own country.

WEBSITES AND INTERNET CAFÉS

There are several Balearic sites you could log on to, including:
www.illesbalears.es highly informative on all aspects
www.mallorca.com general information
www.tomallorca.com rural tourism properties
www.aena.es Palma airport information
www.turismejove.com for students and young travellers
There are Internet cafés in all the resorts. A couple of good ones in Palma are: Azul, Carrer Soledad 4; L@Red Cybercafé, Carrer Concepció 5. Soller: Internet Café, Carrer Luna. Porto Cristo: Academia, Carrer Sementera 43. Alcúdia: Es Canyar, Carrer Major 2.

YOUTH HOSTELS (Albergues juveniles)

There are numerous youth hostels in Mallorca, but it's wise to reserve in advance. A couple of good ones are: Hostel Calma, Carrer Teodoro Canet 25, Puerto Alcúdia; Hostal Oliver, Carrer Bernareggi 37, Cala Figuera (near Mondrago Natural Parc). Most hostels offer single and double rooms as well as dormitories; and can be booked online: www.hostelsweb.com/cities/mallorca.html.

Recommended Hotels

There is a wide range of accommodation available, from luxury hotels to small, family-run hostels, as well as huge, impersonal, but usually very efficient modern hotels in the bigger resorts, where much of the accommodation is block-booked by tour companies. There is also a growing number of small, stylish hotels in inland towns, many of which are delightful. Some hotels close for a few months in winter, so finding inexpensive off-season accommodation isn't always easy. This will be indicated in the listings below. For details on rural *(agroturismo)* holidays and staying in hermitages and sanctuaries, see page 114.

Some rates include breakfast and IVA, the 7 percent value-added tax, but it is not standard, so it is wise to check. The following guide indicates prices for a standard double room in high season (prices should be used as an approximate guide only):

€€€€	over 250 euros
€€€	125–250 euros
€€	75–125 euros
€	below 75 euros

PALMA

Almudaina €€ *Avinguda Jaume III 9, tel: 971 727 340, fax: 971 722 599, www.hotelalmudaina.com.* Comfortable and moderately priced, with obliging staff, the Almudaina is on Palma's foremost shopping street. Established in 1972, it was completely renovated 20 years later. Rooms on upper floors have magnificent views.

Born €€ *Carrer Sant Jaume 3, tel: 971 712 942, fax: 971 718 618, www.hotelborn.com.* In a restored 16th-century palace just off Plaça Rei Joan Carles II, this hotel is one of Palma's best bargains. With a grand central staircase and beautiful courtyard under Romanesque-style arches, it is full of atmosphere. Though not in the luxury league, the rooms are charming and very comfortable. Substantial breakfast, served in the courtyard. Understandably popular, so advance reservations are essential.

Ca Sa Padrina €€ *Carrer Tereses 2, tel: 971 425 300, fax: 971 719 708, www.casapadrina.com.* An attractive hotel furnished in keeping with the converted 19th-century building in which it is set. No breakfast, but there are plenty of nearby cafés.

Convent de la Missió €€€ *Carrer de la Missió 7, tel: 971 227 347, fax: 971 227 348, www.conventdelamissio.com.* This stylish hotel, in a converted 17th-century convent in the old quarter, has light, airy rooms, a roof terrace, solarium and steam rooms and an excellent restaurant.

Dalt Murada €€ *Carrer Almudaina 6, tel: 971 425 300, fax: 971 719 708, www.hoteldaltmurada.com.* In a restored manor house close to the cathedral (the name means 'high walls'), this attractive little hotel has a friendly atmosphere, a garden and wood-panelled entrance hall. Advance reservations recommended.

Hotel III Tres €€€ *Carrer Apuntadors 3, tel: 971 717 333, fax: 971 717 372, www.hoteltres.com.* An elegant hotel with a palm tree reaching up from the lovely old courtyard, a sleek bar, ultra-smart bathrooms and a rooftop terrace with a splash pool.

Palacio Ca Sa Galesa €€€€ *Miramar 8, tel: 971 715 400, fax: 971 721 579, www.palaciocasagalesa.com.* Housed in a grand, meticulously restored 17th-century palace, this tiny hotel (only 12 rooms) is furnished with antiques, has a courtyard with fountain, and the only indoor pool in the old town. Wheelchair access.

Palau Sa Font €€€ *Carrer Apuntadors 38, tel: 971 712 277, fax: 971 712 618, www.palausafont.com.* A delightful hotel in a 16th-century episcopal palace; 19 individually decorated rooms – those at the back are quieter, but this is the quiet end of the busy street.

San Lorenzo €€€–€€€€ *Carrer San Lorenzo 14, tel: 971 728 200, fax: 971 711 901, www.hotelsanlorenzo.com.* This enchanting little hotel (only 6 rooms) is always booked well in advance. Excellent value, rooms individually decorated; all have balconies, some have garden access. Small pool.

THE WESTERN CORNER

Banyalbufar

Baronia € *Carrer Major s/n, tel/fax: 971 618 146, fax: 971 148 738, www.hbaronia.com.* This endearingly simple hotel, set among terraced hills, was part of a 17th-century baronial tower. The rooms are a little spartan, but adequate; all have terraces. Closed Nov–Apr.

Mar i Vent €€ *Carrer Major 49, tel: 971 618 000, fax: 971 618 201, www.hotelmarivent.com.* Attractive family-owned hotel atop a cliff with restaurant, terrace, garden and pool. It has comfortable rooms and stunning sea views. A path leads down to two quiet coves. Also does half board. Closed December–January.

Illetes

Bon Sol €€€ *Paseo de Illetas 30, tel: 971 402 111, fax: 971 402 559, www.ila-chateau.com/bonsol.* A family-run, antique-filled hotel on multiple levels, cascading down pine-shaded cliffs to its own beach. Restaurant, sun terraces, gym. Closed mid-Nov–mid-Dec.

Portals Nous

Bendinat €€€€ *Carrer Andres Ferret Sobral 1, tel: 971 675 725, fax: 971 677 276, www.hotelbendinat.es.* A mid-sized and handsome hacienda-style hotel in a small, rocky cove in this exclusive area. There are rooms with balconies and bungalows amid terraced gardens. Close to five golf courses. Closed Nov–Feb.

Port d'Andratx

Brismar €–€€ *Almirante Riera Alemany 6, tel: 971 671 600, fax: 971 671 183.* This comfortable and simple seafront hotel is a bargain given the coveted location. Ask for a room with a view of the harbour, although these are the noisiest. Wheelchair access.

THE WEST COAST

Deià

Es Molí €€€€ *Carretera Valldemossa–Deià s/n, Deià, tel: 971 639 000, fax: 971 639 333, www.esmoli.com.* Elegant hotel in a 19th-century manor just outside Deià, with incomparable views of the village and the sea. The pool is spring-fed, and the hotel is set in 1.5 hectares (4 acres) of gardens. The service is splendid. Breakfast on the terrace. The highly recommended restaurant, Ca'n Quet, has its own garden. Closed Nov–mid-Apr.

Hostal Villa Verde €€ *Carrer Ramón Llull, Deià, tel: 971 639 037, fax: 971 639 485, www.hostalvillaverde.com.* A simple, friendly little place with a family atmosphere, situated close to the church, with a delightful garden/terrace. Closed Dec–Feb.

La Residencia €€€€ *Son Moragues, Deià, tel: 971 636 046/971 639 011, fax: 971 639 370, www.hotellaresidencia.com.* Elegant hotel, owned by Virgin boss Richard Branson, superbly located in two 16th-century manor houses. A chic international clientele enjoys a health centre, beautiful pools, tennis courts, and El Olivo, one of the island's finest restaurants *(see page 109).*

Miramar €€ *Carrer Ca'n Oliver s/n, Deià, tel/fax: 971 639 084, www.pensionmiramar.com.* Set above the main road up a narrow track, this pleasant little *hostal* has a cavernous entrance hall and rooms with and without bathrooms. Breakfast, which is included in the price, is served on the terrace. Cash only.

S'Hotel d'es Puig €€–€€€ *Es Puig 4, Deià, tel: 971 639 409, fax: 971 639 210, www.hoteldespuig.com.* Tucked away on the stone streets of Deià this delightful little hotel has airy rooms, a serve-yourself bar and a relaxed, friendly atmosphere. Also has four apartments to let in a nearby house, and tenants can use hotel pool. Closed mid-Nov–Feb.

Port de Sóller

Es Port €€ *Antonio Montis s/n, Port de Sóller, tel: 971 631 650, fax: 971 631 662, www.hotelesport.com.* The most attractive hotel in the port, with lovely gardens, sun terraces and great views. Set a few hundred metres back from the beach this 17th-century manor house has beamed ceilings and beautifully furnished rooms. There's a huge olive press in the bar. Heated pools, thalassotherapy service.

Sóller

Ca n'Aí Hotel Rural €€€ *Camí de Son Sales 50 (Cta Sóller– Deià), Sóller, tel: 971 632 494, fax: 971 631 899, www.canai.com.* Family-run for generations, this restored manor house with beams and whitewashed walls is set in orange groves, with canals running through the grounds; 11 suites with terraces. Closed Nov–Feb.

El Guía €€ *Carrer Castanyer 2 Sóller, tel: 971 630 227, fax: 971 632 634.* This pleasant, down-to-earth hotel offers excellent value. Attractive courtyard and a good restaurant that serves typical Malloran dishes. Near the railway station. Closed Nov–Apr.

Gran Hotel Soller €€€€ *Carrer Romaguera 18, Sóller, tel: 971 638 686, fax: 971 631 476, www.granhotelsoller.com.* Sheer luxury, gourmet restaurant and prices to match in this 5-star establishment.

S'Ardeviu €€ *Carrer Vives 14, tel: 971 638 326, fax: 971 638 315, www.sollernet.com/sardeviu.* A comfortable and attractive hotel with just seven rooms and a pretty garden. It's a peaceful spot in a narrow street, although it's close to the vibrant Plaça Major.

Valldemossa

Hotel Valldemossa €€€€ *Ctra Vieja de Valldemossa s/n, tel: 971 612 626, fax: 971 612 625, www.hotelvalldemossa.net.* On the outskirts of town, surrounded by orange and olive groves, this luxurious hotel is set in two 19th-century stone houses, converted and opened in 2004, the rooms furnished with antiques and artworks.

THE NORTH

Alcúdia

Ca'n Simó €€ *Carrer Sant Jaume 1, tel: 971 549 260, fax: 971 549 265, www.cansimo.com.* Bare stone walls, exposed beams and an attractive courtyard give this small hotel, in a converted 19th-century manor house, its character, while smart bathrooms, attractively furnished rooms and an excellent restaurant cater for all creature comforts. For an extra €20 a night you get your own Jacuzzi.

Sant Jaume €€ *Carrer Sant Jaume 6, tel: 971 549 419, fax: 971 897 255, www.hotelsantjaume.com.* Located close to the city walls, this hotel occupies a 19th-century 'Casa Señorial', furnished in keeping with the period. Rooms (there are only six) are individually decorated. It has a pretty patio with a fountain, and an open fireplace to cheer up winter evenings. Closed Dec–Jan.

Cala Sant Vicenç

Cala Sant Vicenç €€€ *Carrer Maressers 2, tel: 971 530 250, fax: 971 532 084, www.hotelcala. com.* Beautifully renovated property in this stunning little bay. Relaxed but extremely efficient. The Cavall Bernat restaurant is recommended. Not suitable for children under 14. Closed Dec–Mar. Wheelchair access.

Hoposa Niu €€€ *Cala Barques s/n, tel: 971 530 100, fax: 971 531 220.* This pleasant, owner-managed hotel overlooking the lovely cove of Cala Sant Vicenç, was upgraded in 2008. Facilities include terraces, bar and an excellent restaurant specialising in fish and lobster. Reserve well in advance. Closed Nov–Mar.

Formentor

Formentor €€€€ *Platja de Formentor s/n, tel: 971 899 100, fax: 971 865 155, www.hotelformentor.net.* This classic hotel was inaugurated in 1929 and guests have included film stars, world leaders and business magnates. The garden terraces are spectacular, as are the beach and views. Three swimming pools, three restaurants, beauty centre. Closed mid-Jan–mid-Feb.

Pollença

Juma €€ *Plaça Major 9, tel: 971 535 002, fax: 971 534 155, www. hoteljuma.com.* This small, smart hotel (only seven rooms), in a *Moderniste* building right on Pollença's picturesque plaza, has been keeping guests happy since 1905. Rooms are comfortable and slightly old-fashioned. Restaurant on the ground floor; breakfast is included. Closed Nov–Dec.

La Posada de Lluc €€€ *Carrer Roser Vell 11, tel: 971 535 220, fax: 971 535 222, www.posadalluc.com.* An elegant, minimalist hotel with a small courtyard, close to the Sant Domingo complex; 8 rooms, individually decorated. Obliging service. Closed Nov–Jan.

L'Hostal €€ *Carrer Mercat 18, tel: 971 535 281, fax: 971 535 282, www.hostalpollensa.com.* Opened in 2005 by the owners of the Juma *(above)*, this 'hotel d'interior' is housed in a traditional town-house, but the large rooms are modern and minimalist, with pale wood and bright colours. Shares reception with the Juma.

Port de Pollença

Miramar €€ *Passeig Anglada Camarasa 39, tel: 971 866 400, fax: 971 864 075, www.hotel-miramar.net.* An attractive, long-established beachfront hotel. The terrace has magnificent views of the bay and Cap de Formentor. Rooms have balconies but not all of them face the beach, so check when you book. Closed Nov–Mar.

Hostal Bahia €€ *Paseo Voramar s/n, tel: 971 866 562, fax: 071 865 630, www.hoposa.es.* An attractive and friendly establishment in a 19th-century summer home, with an inviting terrace, right by the sea. Closed Nov–Feb.

Sins Pins €€ *Passeig Anglada Camarasa 77, tel: 971 867 050, fax: 971 866 264.* This pretty, green-shuttered hotel with friendly staff is right on the beach. The bad news is that many rooms, especially those with sea-view balconies, are booked by tour operators or repeat customers. Worth a try, though.

THE EAST & SOUTHEAST

Artà

Ca'n Moragues €€€ *Carrer Pou Nou 12, Artà, tel: 971 829 509, fax: 971 829 530, www.canmoragues.com.* An 18th-century house tastefully converted into a pleasant hotel, with just eight rooms and an attractive courtyard; 10 percent discount from Nov–Mar.

Casal d'Artà €€ *Carrer Rafael Blanes 19, tel/fax: 971 829 163.* A small family-run hotel in the centre of town opposite a shady square.

Some *Moderniste* features, including good stained glass. Some rooms have four-poster beds. Solarium and roof terrace.

Sant Salvador €€€ *Carrer Castellet 7, Artà, tel: 971 829 555, fax: 971 829 598, www.santsalvador.com.* A 19th-century manor house in the upper town with a *Moderniste* exterior; each of the eight bedrooms is furnished in individual style. Several golf courses nearby. The restaurant, Ca'n Epifanio, is highly regarded *(see page 109)*.

Cala d'Or
Cala d'Or €€ *Avinguda Bélgica 33, tel: 971 657 249, fax: 971 659 351, www.hotelcalador.com.* Attractively situated amid pine trees, this elegant hotel overlooks an almost private cove. It has an established reputation, friendly staff, and all the facilities you would expect. Excellent value. Closed Nov–Easter.

Cala Figuera
Villa Sirena € *Carrer Virgen del Carmen 37, tel: 971 645 303, fax: 971 645 106, www.hotelvillasirena.com.* A good value modern hotel right by the sea at the edge of this pretty village. Closed Nov–Mar.

Cala Ratjada
Cala Ratjada € *Carrer Miguel Garau 2, tel: 971 563 202, fax: 971 818 025, www.hostalcalaratjada.com.* A pleasant little *hostal* right by the port, with bright yellow shutters; en suite rooms, some with small balconies; friendly proprietor. Good budget choice.

Porto Colom
Hostal Porto Colom € *Carrer Cristófol Colom 5, tel: 971 825 323, fax: 971 825 583, www.hostalportocolom.com.* Situated right by the port, this pleasant hotel in an ochre-coloured building offers comfortable accommodation, very reasonably priced.

Ses Rotges €€€ *Carrer Rafael Blanes 21, Cala Ratjada, tel: 971 563 108, fax: 971 564 345, www.sesrotges.com.* An oasis of calm in this busy resort, operated by a husband and wife team. The excellent restaurant has earned a Michelin star. Unsuitable for small children. Closed mid-Nov–mid-Mar, but open for Christmas and New Year.

Binissalem

Scott's Hotel €€€ *Plaça del Església, tel: 971 870 100, fax: 971 870 267, www.scottshotel.com.* An elegant and comfortable English-run hotel in an 18th-century mansion. Large beds and pure cotton sheets are among the pleasures. Minimum stay 3 nights. There's a well-regarded restaurant, Scott's Bistro, tel: 971 870 076.

Randa

Es Reco de Randa €€€–€€€€ *Carrer Font 21 (4km/2½ miles from Algaida), tel: 971 660 997, fax: 971 662 558, www.esrecoderanda. com.* A delightful rural hotel in a manor house, just east of Palma. Exceptional restaurant. Views are excellent, too. Book well in advance as it is popular.

Sineu

Celler de Ca'n Font € *Sa Plaça 18, tel: 971 520 295, fax: 971 520 301, www.canfont.com.* Just 7 rooms, simple, comfortable and air-conditioned, in this old house, which runs a good restaurant.

León de Sineu €€€ *Carrer dels Bous 129, tel: 971 520 211, fax: 971 855 058, www.hotel-leondesineu.com.* An elegant, antique-furnished hotel, close to the central square in this attractive old town. Large, airy rooms. There's a welcoming atmosphere and a good restaurant, Sa Boveda, and the pool is in a shady garden.

Sa Bassa Rotja €€€ *Finca Son Orell, Camino Sa Pedrera s/n, Porreres, tel: 971 168 225, fax: 971 166 563, www.sabassarotja. com.* A 13th-century country mansion set in large grounds, with sports facilities and a restaurant using locally produced ingredients. Ideal for a relaxed short break.

Son Bernadinet €€€ *Carretera Campos–Porreres Km 5.9, tel: 971 650 694, fax: 971 651 340, www.son-bernadinet.com.* A lovely manor house hotel, surrounded by almond orchards, with its own vegetable gardens, and a log fire to warm you in winter. It feels miles from anywhere, but it's only 15 minutes' drive to the nearest beach.

INDEX

Berlitz pocket guide

Mallorca

Third Edition 2011
Reprinted 2012

Written by Pam Barrett
Principal photographer Greg Gladman
Series Editor: Tom Stainer

Photography credits
Greg Gladman 4TR, 4TC, 5BR, 8 13, 14, 16, 18, 23, 26, 28, 29, 31, 32, 33, 34, 35, 36, 38, 41, 43, 44, 45, 46, 48, 49, 50, 51, 53, 57, 58, 59, 61, 62, 66, 67, 71, 73, 75, 77, 79, 82, 85, 86, 89, 95, 96, 105; Chris Coe 20; Glyn Genin 12, 15, 24, 63, 65, 68, 80, 87 103; Britta Jaschinski 11, 19, 39, 55, 93, 99, 104; Neil Schlect 2TR, 10; iStockphoto.com 4BL, 69, 91, 100; Superstock 2BR

Cover picture: 4Corners Images

Every effort has been made to provide accurate information in this publication, but changes are inevitable. The publisher cannot be responsible for any resulting loss, inconvenience or injury.

Contact us

At Berlitz we strive to keep our guides as accurate and up to date as possible, but if you find anything that has changed, or if you have any suggestions on ways to improve this guide, then we would be delighted to hear from you.

Berlitz Publishing, PO Box 7910, London SE1 1WE, England
email: berlitz@apaguide.co.uk
www.berlitzpublishing.com